𝒯𝒽ℯ **Intimacy, Purpose** 𝒶𝓃𝒹 **Power** 𝑜𝒻 **Prayer**

∞ Garfield Crumbie ∾

𝒟ivine { } 𝒲ord
𝒥mpact

ii

The Journey into His Presence

"Upon arrival, I prostrate my spirit before His throne and say nothing.

... I often leave from His throne without ever asking the Father for anything."

Published by Divine Word Impact

ISBN: 978-1-7337554-0-5 (Paperback)
ISBN: 978-1-7337554-1-2 (E-Book)

All scriptures are taken from the KJV version of the bible, except for where specified. Direct quotes from the scriptures are in quotation and are italicized. Nouns that refer to the Father are capitalized.

Other versions of the bible referenced in the text:
The Amplified Version (AMP)
The New International Version (NIV)
The New King James Version (NKJV)

This book is intended to bring the reader into a new consciousness concerning prayer. The results that you receive is solely dependent on you grasping the truths discussed in this book and developing that transformed mind that God's word encourages us to have in order to live His perfect will.

TABLE OF CONTENTS

Chapter 1

Laying the Foundation

ne day Jesus' disciples asked him "LORD, teach us to pray, as John also taught his disciples" (Luke 11:1).

Wouldn't it have been a great experience to have had Jesus himself teach you how to approach the Father in prayer? However, since we were not there, He did not return to the Father without leaving us a roadmap, a blueprint, or a pattern, as to how to communicate with the Father. For many Christians, prayer has become a mundane, boring or a tedious task to do each day. However, it was meant to be a fulfilling, enriching and empowering time, spent in the presence of the Father. In order for us to grow in our relationship with Him, prayer must become a core function of every believer's life, who desires to become a disciplined follower of Christ.

There are several scriptures which tells us that Jesus' disciples were with Him when He went to pray. The first two examples are Matthew 26:36-39 and Luke 9:18. In these passages, He took them with Him, but He was the only one engaged in prayer. We also find that at other times, Jesus would send away His disciples, or the people first, before He went into prayer. Some of the scriptures that states where He prayed in private are listed below.

The Intimacy, Purpose and Power of Prayer

In Matthew 14:22-23, we read that after sending His disciples away into a ship, and then dismissing the crowds, Jesus went up to the mountain by Himself to pray, *"and when the evening was come, he was there alone"*.

Mark 1:35 tells us that *"in the morning, rising up a great while before day, he went out, and departed into a solitary place, and there he prayed"*. There is no mention here of His disciples being with Him.

In Luke 5:15-16, we are told that after the people came out to hear Jesus, and also to bring their sick to be healed by Him, He afterward withdrew Himself into the wilderness, and prayed.

Luke 6:12-13 tells us that Jesus went out into the mountain to pray, and continued all night in prayer to God.

In all the passages that were just mentioned, the one thing that they all have in common is the inference and implication that prayer is a personal and intimate act.

Prayer is practiced in one form or another by myriads of religions around the world. For them, it is their way of getting the attention of their worshipped deity. It may include a variation of ritualistic and ceremonial practices. It is how they manipulate, appease, or invoke their "gods." This practice is

Laying the Foundation

for the purpose of good fortune, protection, and a number of other reasons. In the Hebraic culture, prayer was taught to the children of Yisrael (Israel), from a very early age. Their prayer language was recited out of the *Shemoneh esreh*, otherwise known as the *Amidah*. This was Yisrael's prayer book. *Shemoneh esreh* literally means "eighteen". It refers to the eighteen different types of prayers that were recited for various reasons and occasions, while standing up. They did this on a daily basis. In modern Judaism, it is called *siddurim*. It includes the *Shema* (Deuteronomy 6:4) and the priestly blessing (Numbers 6:24-26). They prayed the written covenant and promises that Elohim made to them, out of the Tanakh, (the Hebrew bible).

Prayer was the life line of Yisrael's relationship with Yahweh, their Elohim. Prayer in the life of New Covenant Believers in Yeshua Hamashiach (Jesus Christ), is more intimate and personal. It is more than just the reciting of words. If we examine Luke 11:1-4, we can arrive at the conclusion that Jesus never spoke to His disciples about prayer up to this point in their walk with Him. He simply lived the life of prayer. On this day, the disciples of Yeshua (Jesus) made a request of Him. They asked Him to teach them how to pray, as how John taught his disciples. There are two questions that come to mind after reading this scripture:

1. *Why did they have to ask Jesus to teach them how to pray?*

The Intimacy, Purpose and Power of Prayer

My assessment of this question is that when the disciples asked Jesus to teach them how to pray, it was like a child asking their parent to love them. It would be a natural tendency, or proclivity for a good parent to show love to their child, thereby teaching them how to love. Our expression of love is an intimate act, and prayer is our intimate expression of love to God. In like manner one would have expected that Jesus would have already taught them how to pray, thereby empowering them to pray.

The simple answer to this question is that the Father will not take us where we are not ready to go, or where we do not express a desire to go. The fact that the disciples asked Him to teach them how to pray, was the expression of that desire.

2. *Why did they not ask Jesus to teach them how to pray as how he prayed, but rather as how John taught his disciples to pray?*

The disciples did not ask Him to teach them how to pray like the Pharisees prayed, or like the other religious sects of their day prayed. They wanted to be taught how to pray, as how John taught his disciples to pray. That request was an expression of a desire that came from them wanting to emulate a good example that they saw in John's disciples.

Laying the Foundation

When we examine this a little closer, we find that it was not really all about prayer, neither was it so much about John and his disciples. It was really about their relationship with Jesus. At the time that this event occurred, John was already dead. However, John's disciples continued to live their lives according to the pattern and blueprint of his teachings. By doing so, they had set an example that drew the attention, and admiration of Jesus' disciples. They were not simply asking for a lesson on how to pray. What they were expressing, was that they wanted to be able to carry on a legacy of Jesus, much in the same way as they had seen John's disciples do with his teaching.

Jesus then, seeing their desire, seized the moment to use the example of John and his disciples, to serve as a foundation on which He would base His narrative of prayer to His disciples. He wanted them to get a vivid and clear demonstration of how they were to be when He was gone. He wanted them to realize how the impact of setting the example would cause others to have the desire and appetite for God.

The scriptures do not provide any specifics or details on John's method of teaching. It is, however, very clear, by virtue of their request, that the disciples had been observing and paying close attention to the life and practices of John's disciples. This, no doubt, made them recognize that something was missing in their traditional prayer life. They saw the far reaching and impacting results of what John did with his disciples.

Even though we are reading this translated account from a Greek perspective, let us remember that the request was made by Hebrews to another Hebrew. The thought process of both the Hebrews and the Greeks, were diametrically opposed to one another. The Hebrews thought in concrete terms and the Greeks thought in abstract terms. In the Hebraic thought process, words were more expressed through concrete concepts and functionality. For example, in describing God, a Hebrew might say "God loves me". This shows a function of God towards man. As for the Greeks, being more consistent with their thought process might say "God is love". Thereby describing God as how they understand him through their intellect.

Let us keep the previous discussion in mind as we consider the phrase "to teach". Every Hebrew letter or word has a concrete image that is attached to it. In Hebrew, the word *Lâmad* (pronounced law-mad'), means to teach and to learn. The image that is connected to the word Lâmad is that of a shepherd's staff, which is used to lead and guide the flock, and to keep them from scattering. It refers to learning by being shown the direction (example Deuteronomy 4:10). The objective of teaching, to the Hebrews, was not the mere relating or disclosing of facts or information.

Another Hebrew word that means to teach is *yada*` (pronounced yaw-dah'). Yada` is to bring you into a personal encounter and experiential knowledge of God. It carries a different nuance from the word *lâmad*. Jesus was pointing them in the direction that would bring them into a personal relationship, and knowledge of the Father. When Jesus was teaching them how to pray, He was not merely giving them information about prayer, He wanted to bring them into the consciousness of who God was to them, and who they were to Him.

We can look at an illustration of this teaching, by looking at the example of two women. They are both capable of giving birth. However, for the woman who have not had the experience of giving birth, she can only get information, or be taught about the process of giving birth. On the contrary, for the woman who has given birth, she learned, or was taught by her experience. Therefore, she was instructed by her own intimate experience. Likewise, when Jesus was teaching His disciples how to pray, He was showing them how to have such an encounter as He experienced in prayer, rather than just giving them information about prayer. It had to do with the personal embrace, and intimate interaction and application of that knowledge.

Shanan (pronounced shaw-nan'), is another Hebrew word for *to teach*. It means to make pointed; or to sharpen, as in the case of a knife or a sword; teach (incisively). It carries the idea or concept of being skilled or competent. (Deuteronomy 6:6-7). The final Hebrew term is the word *yarah* (pronounced yaw-raw'). It literally means to throw; cast; shoot (1 Samuel 20:20). It also refers figuratively to the "throwing of the finger". The implication here means to point (Exodus 15:24-25). It can be understood to mean to "learn by pointing out the way." What the disciples were really asking Yeshua to do for them, was for Him to point out the way in which they were to make their approach to God, to make them skilled and competent in the way of Yahweh, and to teach them the language of Elohim, which is prayer. The Hebrews believed that knowledge was intimate and personal, which upon reception and application, would have transforming, life changing, and far reaching ramifications. That is really what they were asking for, when they asked Jesus to teach them how to pray.

Chapter 2

What is Prayer?

*B*efore we can proceed any further on the subject of prayer, it is really important that we understand the concept and dynamics of prayer. It is absolutely necessary for us to grasp the gravity, the value, and the mandate to pray. The first order of things is to define the practice of prayer, and the role it plays in the life of a New Covenant Believer. The one million dollar question is, "what is prayer?"

There are those who view prayer as a religious right that must be done. There are those who see it as a laborious task that they have to push, pull, and force themselves to do. Others see it as a seven or twelve-step set of principles, that once they have accomplished it, they're good to go. There are "spiritual" folks who have their "times of prayer", but no consistent and disciplined life of prayer. For these folks, when they are in trouble, it is their times of prayer. When they are in lack, it is their times of prayer. When they are sick, it is their times of prayer. There are others who are too busy, and only pray on the go, (I call these microwave prayers), but spend no quality time in prayer. These are wrong ways to approach prayer.

The Intimacy, Purpose and Power of Prayer

Prayer is the foundation for building an intimate relationship with the Father. It is having communion with both the Father and His son Jesus (1 John 1:3). Prayer is not just an expression of the intellect, saying beautifully words. Rather, prayer is the engagement of the intellect (the mind)

and the spirit man, whereby we use the intellect to communicate what the spirit man is relating to the Spirit of God. There are times however, when it is just the spirit man communicating with the Spirit of God. Our mind may not understand it, but our spirit is being enlarged by what we receive from God's Spirit. For we pray with the spirit and with the understanding also (1 Corinthians 14:15).

Prayer is Communication

*T*here are clichés that are used as clever little lines to talk about prayer. "If you pray, you will stay." "One week without prayer, makes one weak." "A family that prays together, stays together." As well intended as these sayings may be, they are just clichés. It is not the mere act of praying that lends the possibility to such outcomes becoming a reality. It is the life changing consequence of fervent and effectual prayer that will bring about these results. On this I have scriptural support. James 5:16 says that *"the effectual fervent prayer of a righteous man availeth much."* Let us examine this scripture.

The word *effectual* in the Greek is the verb *energeo* (pronounced *en-erg-eh'-o*). It means to put forth power; to be operative; be at work. It can also be interpreted to mean yielding results. The word *fervent* is from the Greek verb *zeo‾* (pronounced dzeh'-o), which means to be hot; to boil with heat. The word *righteous* is a legal term in the Greek. It means to be in good or right standing. A person who is a law abiding citizen, is a person, who by the legal term of the law, would be considered righteous. *Avail* means to help or benefit. The combination of these words then yield the interpretation, that prayer will profit or benefit much, when it is put forth with power, or made operative (used with skill), with hot or intense zeal. But we must also be in right standing or right relationship with the Father.

Prayer is intimate and personal communication with the Father. Communication is the building block of human relations and interaction on any level, whether it is professional, platonic or intimate. The word for communicate in Greek, koinōneō (pronounced koy-no-neh'-o), means to come into communion or fellowship with; to become a sharer; be made a partner. Therefore, communication can be defined as the sharing of one's self and intentions, by way of action or vocalization. Communication also connotes connection. It is possible for communication to occur in only one direction. In this case it is a uni-directional connection. When it occurs in both directions, it is a bi-directional connection. Unfortunately, for a lot of believers, their prayers are uni-directional. In most of these cases, the communication is from them to God, telling Him all that their heart desires and wishes, and the needs that they have to be met. They fail to allow God to return the communication, where He can speak His peace into them, impart His wisdom, bring them into greater understanding, and reveal His plan.

Our communication with God comes with a certain protocol. A protocol is the terms of agreement made beforehand, or the official procedure as to how an action is taken. When Jesus gave His disciples instruction on how to pray, He was not telling them to repeat the same words that He did and then conclude that they have prayed. Rather, He was giving them a template that they should follow as they prayed. Jesus began by saying *"Our Father which art in Heaven, ..."* Luke 11:2. This was to be received as the protocol that should be followed as to how we should approach God. In going to God, we must first know who it is that we are approaching, what His relationship is to us, and where it is that we are meeting Him.

"Our Father" signifies who it is that we are approaching and the nature of the relationship we have with Him. When we say "who art in Heaven", this is us proclaiming that we understand that He resides in a place of power, authority and might. This reinforces to us what His abilities are, and the caliber of "person" with whom we are about to share our selves. Therefore, the protocol that we should follow in approaching God simply states that we should approach Him in a certain state of consciousness.

The extent or degree of sharing one's self, or things with another, is predicated on the nature of the relationship, and the level of "security clearance", or access that one person allows in the life of the other. In the realm of human affairs and interaction, communication does not only initiate relationships, but it is also needed to build and sustain it. The level of access that you give God in your life, determines the level of influence that He can have with you. James 4:8 says that if we *"draw nigh to God,"* He will in turn *"draw nigh to"* us. This tells us then, that the depth, or the degree to which we openly share ourselves with God, will determine the level of intimacy we experience in our communication with Him. This understanding alone should underscore, reinforce, and drive home the important role of communication.

In order for us to engage in fruitful communication on any level, there are three core areas about a person that we need to understand or be aware of. These core areas includes their history, their language and their philosophy. Their history has to do with where they are coming from. Their language has to do with how they communicate. Their philosophy has to do with their worldview. When we understand that our Father's history in dealing with man has been that of mercy, goodness, grace, long suffering, love, etc., it becomes easier for us to trust Him. When we understand that His philosophy of us is that even though He knew man was in a destitute, vagabond and deplorable sinful state, and He still looked at us and loved us to the point where He said "they are still worth saving". It then becomes easier for us to love Him back. We can also then believe, and accept, that His thoughts of us are of peace and not evil, to give us an expected end (Jeremiah 29: 11). When we understand His language, and how to communicate with Him, it will inspire us to boldly approach His Throne of Grace, both on the merit of the righteousness that He imputed to us, and on the merit of who He is.

Prayer is Intimate

*P*rayer is the time of intimate sharing. It is the time when you intimately share yourself with the Father, and He intimately shares Himself with you. It is a time of close fellowship and communion between your spirit and the Father's Spirit. The word for share in the Greek is *koinonia* (pronounced koy-nohn-ee'-ah). It speaks of the thing that is shared in common as the basis of fellowship. It stresses the relational aspect of the fellowship. The word *intimacy* is derived from the Latin word *intimare*, which means "impress," or "make familiar". *Intimare* is derived from the Latin root *intimus*, which means "inmost." The word *impress* means to make a mark or design on (an object) using a stamp or seal; to make an imprint; an act of making an impression or mark. The word familiar means in close friendship. As human beings, when we spend time with each other, we usually leave a measure of influence on each other. Likewise, when we spend time with the Father in prayer, we share our love with Him, and He impresses His mark on the table of our heart. That which He shares with us, will affect our innermost being. The impact of what He deposits in our spirit, in these precious moments, will be realized in our spiritual growth and maturity in Him.

Some of the areas of our lives that this will be manifested in is our sense of judgment, discernment, our decision making and how we relate to other people.

Chapter 3

Our Prayer Language

*S*eeing that I have established that prayer is intimate communication with the Father. It is therefore, necessary that I also establish what the language of this communication is. You may have experienced a time when someone was speaking with you, but you didn't fully understand what they were saying, because their native language was different from your own. They may have used some words in their language that were familiar to you, but you did not get the full message that they were trying to communicate to you, because you were not fully versed in or knowledgeable about the entire language. We would say that there was a "language barrier" between you and that person. It is said that communication is about getting the message out. If you cannot understand the language, you most certainly will not get the message.

For us to become fluent in speaking a language, we must learn the words that make up the language. The make-up of verbal or written communication are words, which when are structured in a meaningful way, makes up language. The result of effective communication is understanding.

The Intimacy, Purpose and Power of Prayer

In order for us to gain understanding or get the message when the Father speaks to us, and for Him to receive our message when we speak to Him, we have to speak the same language. The common language between us and the Father is made up of His Word in the Holy Scriptures. The book that contains His Word, the bible, then serves as our "prayer book."

Elohim told Joshua, in Joshua 1:8 that *"this book of the law shall not depart out of thy mouth."* God was letting Joshua know that the language of his prayers were to be made up of the Word from the Book of The Covenant. God also instructed Joshua to meditate on His word day and night. In other words, God was telling Joshua to become well versed in His Word, whereby he would become fluent in His (God's) language. Your understanding of the Word is what increases your prayer language. When you pray what the Father has already said in His Word, you are effectively speaking His language and declaring His will. This will guarantee that He will get the message of your prayer.

Yeshua told His disciples in the book of John 15:7, that *"If ye abide in me, and my words abide in you, ye shall ask what ye will, and it shall be done unto you."* He was not saying that He was giving them a blank check to ask for whatsoever they wanted. He qualified it by saying *"If ye abide in me, and my words abide in you"*. His word abides in us through meditation. The word "abide" in English means to accept, or act in accordance with. In Greek, to abide is the word *menó*, which means to stay; abide; remain. Therefore, if we accept the sovereignty of God, and act according to His word, it is inevitable that He will respond to our request. That's because we will be asking according to His word that stays/remains in us, and not according to our selfish and imperfect will. The point here is that, His abiding word will become the expressed language of our prayers, thus ensuring answered prayers, because He cannot deny His word. This is according to Numbers 23:19, Psalm 138:2, Hebrews 6:13-18.

The Intimacy, Purpose and Power of Prayer

Chapter 4

Relationship with God

*W*e dealt with prayer in the sense of how to speak to the Father, in terms of telling Him what we are in need of, or our expectation of Him. We discussed how prayer is intimate communication with the Father. This aspect of prayer is both faith and word based. Let us now take a look at another side of prayer. That is, the relationship oriented side of prayer. This aspect of prayer is also word and faith based.

It is possible to want something from a person, but yet not want to have any type of relationship, interaction, or personal association or connection with them. I found it very needful to address this, because so often we are pre-occupied with praying to the Father for things, that we lightly esteem seeking Him for who He is. The relationship oriented side of prayer seeks to build relationship with the Father beyond what we can get from Him.

What is relationship? What does it really mean? Relationship can be defined as "a joint partnership between two parties of common or related interest". This word comes from the Greek word *koinonia*, which we discussed earlier in describing our communion with God. We made mention that its meaning stresses the relational aspect of the fellowship. We further note here, that it is used as a descriptive term in reference to the bond of marriage. It conveys the idea of a powerful common interest that could hold two or more persons together. Up until the coming, and the death of Christ, God and man had no powerful common interest that could have brought us together, or keep us together. There was nothing that could create a marital bond or union between God and man.

From the Greek perspective, fellowship is defined as sharing, partaking, communion, and intercourse. It conveys the idea of sharing with a person "in something." That thing which the two parties share, becomes the common ground that binds or attach them together. The word *intercourse* means intimate connection or dealings between persons, groups or nations. It means interchange of thoughts, feelings, communication of ideas, and entrance. Ephesians 5:22-25 makes reference of a husband and wife as being a representation, or a type of Christ and His bride, (the church), both in terms of the marriage covenant and intimate relationship. The parallel that can be drawn between Christ and the church, and a husband and wife, as relating to intimacy, can be described with the following illustration.

Relationship with God

When a husband and wife become intimate, the process of reproduction can only occur if entrance is given, by which the seed of the promise of a new birth, is released. After this seed (spermatozoon) is released, it makes its journey to the egg cell (ovum) of the wife, which when is pierced by the spermatozoon, causes fertilization to occur. When the ovum gets fertilized, the surface of the egg changes, preventing another spermatozoon from entering. At the time of fertilization, the genetic makeup becomes complete. This genetic makeup is what determines, (among other things), whether the baby will be male or female (Webmd.com).

The spiritual parallel to the illustration that was just described, is that when we go into prayer, we as the bride of Christ should allow ourselves to be completely open to the Father. We should not withhold any part of ourselves as we enter into a time of intimate communion with Him. This will allow the seed of faith, the seed of breakthrough, the seed of transformation, and other such seeds, to penetrate the ovum of our spirit, thereby causing us to become pregnant with our destiny or the hidden power that will determine what will be born out of us, in the process of time. Because His thoughts towards us is that of peace and not evil, so that He can give us an expected end, the seed that He implants in us, already have the genetic makeup, or DNA necessary to bring forth the fruit of our destiny. Those thoughts, are that which He thought toward us, even before He "knew" us, or engaged us in fellowship. As Jeremiah 1:5 says, *"Before I formed thee in the belly I knew thee; ...*" The word *knew* in Hebrew, carries the idea of having intimate relationship.

The ovum can be seen with our naked eye, but a spermatozoon can only be seen when magnified. When the Father deposits His seed of faith and destiny in us, it is not apparent to those that are on the outside. However, we will know that we have received a deposit in our spirit from the Father, because we sense the change as time progresses. It is only when a natural baby comes to a certain point of maturity that others begin to see that the mother is carrying or expecting. The spiritual parallel of this is that when our faith starts to grow, and our destiny begins to form, others will notice. It does not yet mean that we are ready to give birth to it, but with the proper nourishment, and by continuing in fellowship with the Father, it will come to full maturity.

In the process of the coming together of a woman's egg (ovum) and the male spermatozoon, it takes time for the spermatozoon to swim towards the ovum. However, the ovum usually does not make much movement after reaching the fallopian tube. It stays in place while the spermatozoon makes its way to it (Webmd.com). The spiritual parallel to this is that if we quit struggling on our own, and remain in our meeting place with the Father, the word that He directs to us, will find us, and impregnate us with the purpose and destiny that He has for us. He will give us an expected end, because He already knows what the end result of our intimate time together will be.

Even though we go before Christ as an individual believer, it is important that we also go in the collective and corporate consciousness of His bride. It is at this level of interaction that we open up ourselves to Him, thus giving Him access and entrance into the deep recess of our spirit, which I call the spirit womb. This is the place that He has created in us to receive Him. It is in this place that He releases His seed. This seed contains His communications to us. It contains His thoughts, His heart, His will, His purpose, His agenda, His ideology, His concept, and His philosophy/worldview. This is the time when we expose who we really are to Him, thus giving Him access, so that He can address and work on those particular areas of our lives that need to be resolved. It is in this place where His Devine DNA, which contains the information of His character, His ways, and His nature, otherwise known as the Fruit of the Spirit in Galatians 5:22-23, are produced by Him, in us. This is so that we may give birth to His traits, character, and attribute outside of us. When we allow this process to run its course, then the life we live will resemble, and bare the image and reflection of the life of His son, Yeshua, when he lived on earth.

The Intimacy, Purpose and Power of Prayer

Chapter 5

Privacy in Prayer

*W*hen a man and a woman, who are of a strong moral compass, want to have a time of intimacy with each other, they find a place that is private and unrevealing. Why? This is because of the nature of such interaction. It calls for such level of privacy. As we reflect on the scriptures that were mentioned in the beginning of this writing, concerning Jesus praying, we can see that they stated that before going into prayer, He would send the multitude and His disciples away, while He went into the mountain or another private place to pray. In some cases He would pray all night by Himself. When we go before God in intimate fellowship, it is important that we understand that such level of intimacy calls for such level of privacy.

Jesus admonished His disciples in Matthew 6:5 that they should not pray like the hypocrites who make a show of their prayers standing in the synagogues and in the corners of the streets. They should instead find a private place to pray to the Father. When we pray, we are not trying to show anyone how spiritual we are, or how well we can articulate our words in prayer. We do not pray to get praise from man, we pray to get results from the Father. It is in this time of privacy that we open ourselves for God to see the innermost parts of us, that we would rather not share with others. This is the time when we can expose those things about us that only the Father can take away and replace with His wholesomeness, thereby transforming us.

When conception occurs after intimacy, it affects the woman's appetite and desire. They may have no desire for certain food or drink, or they may have cravings for strange things. Not only is their sense of taste and smell affected, but their mood may also sway from time to time. Some lifestyle changes may also have to be made. As her body begins to change, it will show the outward physical evidence of the intimacy that brought about all those changes. The most dynamic changes, however, are the ones that takes place on the inside of her. One particular change that I want to focus on, is the change that takes place with the heart. During this period, the "blood volume increases by 30-50 percent, and the heart pumps more blood by the minute, and the heart rate increases" (*Mayo Clinic*). When we spend time in the bedchamber of His Presence in quality intimacy, and allow Him to release His seed into the womb of our spirit, we will leave from that communion carrying something in our womb. It is that something that will affect our appetite and desire for Him. It will cause changes and transformation to begin to take place on the inside of us. It will affect our behavior, attitude, and character. It will affect our decision making process. In other words, it will have a great impact on our heart. Over a period of time, those internal changes will begin to show on the outside. With the fullness of time, we will give birth to the image and likeness of the Christ seed, that according to Galatians 4:19, which is forming in us.

When the Christ seed in us have been fully formed, and we have morphed into the image of Christ, He will be the one that will speak through us and we will not have to give thought as to what to answer when we are asked about the hope that we have in us. In Acts 4:13-14, the scripture gives an example of what we will be like when Christ is fully formed in us. In this scripture, Peter and John were detained for preaching *"through Jesus the resurrection from the dead"* (Acts 4:2). They were asked to defend under what authority they spoke the things that they did. After Peter spoke, they were confounded by what they heard, because as the scripture said, they *"perceived that they were unlearned and ignorant men."* They also took note that they had been with Jesus. The point is, when Christ has been formed in us, through the time that we spend with Him, we will not have to speak anything of our own accord. The fully mature Christ in us will speak through us. We will not have to defend ourselves, because the Father will present the evidence that will shut the mouth of the naysayers. The proof of this scripture is in verse 14 that says *"And beholding the man which was healed standing with them, could say nothing against it."*

The Intimacy, Purpose and Power of Prayer

We should not think of our journey with Christ as living for Him. That puts us in the consciousness of us putting forth our own effort. We should instead view it in the correct way, which according to Galatians 2:20 says *"Christ liveth in me"*. This puts the onus on the one who is now living, the Christ.

During our time of intimacy with the Father, it is not the time to make need oriented requests. During this time, you don't talk about bills in the bedchamber, you don't talk about you in the bedchamber. The focus, attention, and affection is on and about the one that you are being intimate with. How would you like to be having some intimate times with your spouse and they are telling you which bills are due, how much the bills are, or "you better talk to your momma". This would mean that one spouse showed up with their whole self, and the other showed up with only half of themself. That would spoil the intimate moment in a heartbeat.

When you enter into the bedchamber of His Presence it must be all of you, because God is showing up with all of Himself. The bible tells us in Genesis 3 that God showed up in the cool of the day to talk to Adam. God showed up with all of Himself, but only half of Adam showed up, because the other part of him was dead (spiritually). The part of Adam that showed up was hiding behind the trees. Do not spoil your intimate moments with God by hiding behind anything in His Presence.

Privacy in Prayer

In times of intimacy between a man and his wife, unclothing themselves allows each person to be completely revealed, with nothing hidden. Allow yourself to be naked and unashamed in God's presence, meaning, be completely vulnerable in His presence, holding nothing back. He also allows Himself to be naked in our presence, by revealing different aspects of Himself to us. The Father reveals His bosom to us, which speaks of His heart. He reveals His hand to us, which speaks of His works. He reveals His face, thereby giving us a level of closeness to Himself. When the scripture speaks of Moses having a face to face interaction with God (Exodus 33:11), the bible says that He spoke with Moses as a man to his friend. This means that during the times that Moses spent with God, his relationship had evolved to another level. At this point, He spoke with Moses not just as a man, but as a friend.

The bible says that our righteousness is as filthy rags in God's sight, and our iniquities as the wind that takes us away (Isaiah 64:6). When we enter into God's presence, we are unclothed of our filthy rags and are clothed with God's grace, compassion and love. The different revealing of ourselves to each other builds a deeper relationship, and forges a greater bond of oneness. It is during those times that God reveals yourself to you. Private prayer allows Him to deal with the core of who we are, and not the surface of who or what we project or portray ourselves to be.

Chapter 6

How Prayer Transforms

*T*he word *transform* in Greek is *metamorphoō (pronounced met-am-or-fo'-o)*. It is a compound of *metá* and *morphoō*. Metá means "change after being with" and morphoō means "changing form in keeping with inner reality." Therefore, metamorphoō literally means "a change or conversion after being with". When we have been with the Father, or have spent intimate times in His presence, we will undoubtedly be changed into a form that is in keeping with who God is.

The bible says in Genesis 1:1 that *"In the beginning .... the earth was without form and void, and darkness was upon the face of the deep. And The Spirit of God moved upon the face of the waters. And God said, let there be light and there was light."* The Hebrew understanding of this scripture is that the Spirit of God hovered over, or brooded upon the face of the deep. When we think of brooding, we think of a hen that sits on her eggs in order to give warmth and protection, until those eggs bring forth life of the same kind, a chicken. This scripture is analogous to Christ nurturing and protecting us, until we are fully formed in His own image.

The Intimacy, Purpose and Power of Prayer

The Spirit of God moved upon the face of the waters, but spoke into its deep. The deep speaks of man's heart. Quality time spent in prayer, allows the deep within us to call out to the deep that God is. When we spend time in the light of His presence, He is able to speak into the dark places of our hearts/deep and bring change and transformation to our life. Up until the time that God spoke into the deep, it was empty and dark. If we do not spend relational time in His presence, the deep of our hearts will become void. We will then yearn for other things to fill it, instead of seeking Him who fills all in all. However, when we spend quality time in the Father's presence, we give Him the opportunity to brood over us, thereby allowing His light to enter into our hearts.

Romans 8:29 says *"For whom he did foreknow, he also did predestinate to be conformed to the image of his Son ...."* The word for *conform* in Greek is *sysxēmatízō* (pronounced soos-khay-mat-id'-zo). Used as a verb, it means to assume a similar outward form (expression) by following the same pattern (model, mold). Another Greek word, *symmorphos* (pronounced sü'm-mor-fos), is used as an adjective, and has the definition "conformed by sharing the same inner essence-identity (form); showing similar behavior from having the same essential nature". This is the form of the word *conform* that is used here in Romans. This scripture speaks of God having a particular purpose in mind for us. His divine will for us, is for us to take on a new identity that will cause us to share or to have the same essential nature as His.

How Prayer Transforms

When we share the same inner essence or identity of the Father, we will begin to think as He thinks. When we are conformed to His image, we take on His mind, which affects our worldview. The scripture says that we should be transformed, by the renewing of our mind (Romans 12:2). To have a transformed mind means to have a changed mind. A changed mind requires a different way of thinking. A different way of thinking produces new thoughts. These new thoughts are filtered through our perception. Our perception is based on what or how we see, or how we become aware of something. When the scripture admonishes us to allow the mind of Christ to be in us (Philippians 2:5), it is telling us to allow God to shape our perception so that we will be able to see things as how He sees them. This will undoubtedly affect how we approach different situations in life. This is how we will grow from faith to faith. In order for us to allow God to change our perception, we have to become aware of what He is aware of. We do this by studying His word.

2 Peter 1:2-4, shows us how this works. Verse 2 says *"Grace and peace be multiplied unto you through the knowledge of God, and of Jesus our LORD."* Our peace is predicated upon our thoughts. Here Peter is saying that our peace will be multiplied, or become greater by what we know of God. For us to know our God, we must read His word and receive revelation knowledge from God. Peter went on to say in verse 3, *"According as his divine power hath given unto us all things that pertain unto life and godliness, through the knowledge of*

him that hath called us to glory and virtue." Again, for us to receive all things that pertain to life and godliness according to God's divine power, it is necessary, not negotiable, that we know the Word of God. Verse 4 says that we are given exceeding great and precious promises, by which we might be partakers of the divine nature. The verses leading up to verse 4 basically states that we obtain these things through the knowledge of God. Therefore, the way that we become partakers of God's divine nature, or become conformed to His image, (which, according to our earlier discussion, means to have the same essential nature), is to study the Word that we may gain knowledge of God. Our knowledge of Him will produce thoughts that brings us peace.

In the beginning, before God spoke into the deep, it was empty and dark. When He spoke His word, the deep was filled with all manner of life form. God wants to speak into the empty and dark areas of our lives, that light and life may spring forth. David said that the entrance of thy word gives light (Psalm 119:130). He also said that thy word have I hid in my heart, that I might not sin against thee (Psalm 119:11). How does the word reach to our heart/deep? By studying the Word and meditating on it. Joshua 1:8 says *"This book of the law shall not depart out of thy mouth; but thou shalt meditate therein day and night, that thou mayest observe to do according to all that is written therein: for then thou shalt make thy way prosperous, and then thou shalt have good success."* By doing this, when we go into prayer, the Father has a foundation from which to speak to us. By knowing His word, we will know His language and therefore, we will be able to understand when He speaks to us. Therefore, the three-fold cord of studying the word, meditating on it and fellowshipping with the Father will create a greater, and stronger bond between us and the Father.

Energy is the ability to do work (Gregersen, E.). It comes in different forms, among which are Heat, Light and Motion (eia.gov). The two types of energy are potential (stored) and kinetic (working) energy. When we have the Word of God in our heart, it is like potential energy that is stored within. It gives the Father a target or a mark within us, which He can strike. When we spend time in prayer, He speaks into our heart/deep and He releases spirit and life (John 6:63). The potential energy of the word that is stored in us, is ignited by the word that God speaks into our deep. This sets His word in motion, (life producing). He releases revelation of His word (light producing), which enable us to become the light of the world, by reproducing what the Father have produced in us.

As we discussed earlier, the Spirit and the Word work together. When the Spirit of God moved, the Word commanded action also. There are Christians who pray more than they read the word, and there are those who read the word more than they pray. However, there needs to be a balance, because they are both equally important. Fellowship with the Father is Word based. When we spend relational time in His presence, it is His word that is already in our hearts that He will use to search our hearts and perform His works. Hebrews 4:12 states that *"The Word of God is quick, (life giving), and powerful, and sharper than any two-edged sword; piercing even to the dividing asunder of soul and spirit, and of the joints and the marrow, and is a discerner of the thoughts and intents of the heart."* The word power in the Greek is *dynamis*, from where we get the word *dynamite.* It means the "ability to perform", "able, having ability." A related word is the adjective *dynatos*, it speaks of what is made possible as a result of the power or ability that is demonstrated by the subject. When we read the word, the power of God is stored in our hearts as potential, or ability to perform. This can be likened to potential energy that is stored in an unused dynamite. When we fellowship with the Father in prayer, His Spirit that broods over us, incubates the Word that is in our hearts, so that it will develop into the thing that He will name or call it. That is, it will ignite the fuel of the Word that is already stored in our hearts as potential energy, to bring it into "word in motion", that is, into kinetic energy (energy in motion). This "word in motion" is what will produce power to perform what God wills it to do. Ephesians 3:20 *"Now unto him that is able to do exceeding abundantly above all that we ask or think, according to the power that worketh in us."* The Spirit and the Word, working together, creates an explosive, life generating force.

In the beginning, before the Spirit of the LORD brooded over the water, the earth was without form and void. That is to say, the earth was in a chaotic state. However, when God began to speak and commanded things "to be", the earth began to take on order, structure and purpose. Likewise, when we come into fellowship with the Father, He is able to bring order, structure and purpose to our lives.

Hebrews 4:12 tells us that the Word of God is life giving, and powerful, and sharper than any two-edged sword, that can divide apart the soul and spirit. In Isaiah 53:12, it states that Jesus poured out his soul unto death. Here the soul is being likened to water. The dry land speaks of the spirit. It is solid, stable and consistent. It is the part of man that God communicates with. The soul is the center of our awareness and human consciousness. This is how we relate to our physical environment. It contains the five senses. Therefore, as God separated the water from the land, his word will create a separation of soul and spirit. Why? So that God can bring order and structure to our lives, so that we will become fruitful or live with intent (purpose). We see the parallel to this at the time of creation, when the earth only brought forth grass, herb yielding seed and fruit tree, after God separated the waters and the earth.

The order that God wants to bring to our lives, is the order in which communication is transmitted through our being, which will dictate who has control. In the beginning, when God created man, He first created the body, then breathed into man, and man became a living soul. Therefore, the order in which we came into being, was body, soul and spirit. In I

Thessalonians 5:23, the scripture says "... *I pray God your whole spirit and soul and body be preserved blameless unto the coming of our LORD Jesus Christ*". What God wants to do, is to reverse the order of control in our lives. In order to put the sin nature, in which we were born, in check, the Spirit has to be the one leading. When we remain in fellowship with God, He communicates to the spirit man, and the spirit then communicates to the soul man. The body is the vehicle of manifestation through which what is being communicated, is made apparent. Therefore, without our continuous fellowship with God in prayer, the soul will be the one that dictates to the spirit, and the body will manifest the desires of the soul. This is why there is a continuous struggle between the soul and the spirit of man. A struggle for control. Galatians 5:17 states that "the flesh lusteth against the spirit, and the spirit against the flesh." In order for us to keep our bodies under the subjection of the Spirit, our spirit has to openly receive from the Father.

Our soul will then come under the control of the Spirit and our bodies will then manifest the intent and purpose of the Father. This will lead to us to being a new man and a new creation in Christ.

Chapter 7

First that which is Natural

*I*n Proverbs 8:29, we are told that when God gave the sea a decree, it was that the waters should not pass His commandment (its boundaries), to inundate the earth. When we live in His presence, His word will create the boundaries in our life so that the soul/water does not overwhelm or dominate the spirit/earth. As a result of living in His presence, the Spirit of God is able to keep us in check.

God's Spirit has kept me in check many times. I remember one day at my job, I hugged a female friend. Afterwards, the Spirit of God said to me that I should not have hugged her the way that I did. He said to me that, that type of hug is for my wife. As I pondered what He had said to me, I saw the wisdom of His counsel. From that point on I have made sure not to do that again.

Another account that I remember, is that one day, after I had just wrapped up a time of fasting, something happened, and I got angry and slammed a cupboard door hard. The Spirit of the LORD said to me, "did you not just finished fasting?" I felt so bad and convicted that I had to repent.

The Intimacy, Purpose and Power of Prayer

On one other occasion, my wife said something to me that made me very upset, to the point that I responded in an aggressive manner. The LORD then said to me that it had nothing to do with her, because I was blaming her for getting upset. He said that it had to do with what was going on inside of me. He said that she would conclude within herself, that if I spend so much time in prayer and in the word, and it has not affected or changed my behavior or attitude, then it does not make sense her praying, because it will not change anything. The LORD gave me insightful understanding that day, that changed me in that regard.

His Spirit is also able to give you direction that will keep you from experiencing devastation in the future. I remember about three years ago, (from the time of this writing), I got up one morning, and the LORD said to me forcefully, "You need to change your diet now." I obeyed and started immediately. A few days later, I asked Him in a kind of annoying tone, "Why am I doing this?" He said that oftentimes He sees a sickness that is about to come upon His people and would warn them. However, because they relegate Him only to spiritual matters, they do not listen. Then when the sickness or disease come upon them, they seek Him for healing. After I heard this, I said to my wife that I would know that this was the LORD speaking to me, because something is going to happen, which will cause me to have to go to the hospital. Then I will know why the LORD gave that instruction to me.

First that which is Natural

About one year or so later, while I was at work sitting at my desk, I felt my head starting to spin. I was wondering to myself what was going on. I felt myself starting to slowly go out like someone who was slowly falling off to sleep. I tried to get up, but I kept falling back into my seat. On my last attempt, I fell back on the wall because I had no balance. Needless to say, I could not stand up. Two of my co-workers had to physically take me to the school nurse because I could not walk. She checked my blood pressure three times. Each time that she checked it, she kept looking at it with a puzzled expression. She said to me that the reason that she kept doing that was because she thought the machine was broken. My pressure was about 241 over 140. She said that in all of her years of being a nurse, she has never seen a reading that high before. I was in what they called the death zone. I was immediately rushed to the hospital in an ambulance.

That night, they tried vigorously to bring down and stabilize my pressure with different medications. My blood pressure persisted at that very high level throughout the night, therefore, I had to be admitted to the inpatient ward. I stayed in the hospital for three days and three nights. The doctors kept asking me if I was feeling any chest pains, had numbness in any of my limbs or had a headache. They were surprised that my response was no to all of the above. I asked the doctor why it was taking so long to bring down and stabilize my pressure. He said that my pressure was very stubborn. He also said that for it to be that stubborn, I had to be living with high blood pressure for at least over ten years. They could not understand why I did not have a heart attack or a stroke.

One day I said to the nurse, that was attending to me, that about a year or so ago I changed my diet and began to eat healthy, so why did this happen. She gave me a two-fold response. She said that if I had not changed my diet at the time that I did, we would most likely not be having that conversation. She also said that unfortunately, I am genetically predisposed to having high blood pressure. After running countless number of tests, they also discovered that I had high cholesterol and type two diabetes. I was prescribed six different medications to take on a daily basis.

I had totally forgotten what the LORD had told me about a year or so prior to this incident. However, as I laid in the hospital bed, He brought it back to my remembrance. My mouth flew open in amazement. All I could do was thank and praise God for giving me the wisdom of obedience. That is why the bible says, hear and your soul shall live. When you live in His presence, He will reveal His heart concerning His will and purpose for you.

He will also reveal your gifting and give you the grace to carry out your assignment. I spent thirty one years of my life living in New York. I attended the same ministry for twenty of those years. One day, the Spirit of the LORD said to me that

First that which is Natural

He has a new place of assignment for my wife and I. It kind of blew me away because the thought of moving anywhere, even more so out of New York, was not within the universe of my thought process. I filed it away in the filing cabinet of my mind and left it there.

Let me double back for a second and give you the full scoop. I worked full time for our ministry for four years. A part of my responsibility was managing the ministry's book store. One day, a lady came into the store and stood for a little while at the showcase. She asked me if I had any plans to move. I said "No". Truth be told, I was also a little annoyed, because the idea of moving was not on my "to do" list. To humor myself, I asked her why she had asked me that question. She said that when she walked in the store and looked at me, she saw me moving to Florida. My response was to just file it away in the filing cabinet of my mind as before, and thought nothing of it again.

About three years later, one of our prophetic intercessors said to me, "Elder I had a dream about you last night." I said "What was the dream?" She told me that she dreamt that I had moved to Florida to accept a promotion. At that point my mind reflected on what the lady in the book store had said to me about three years earlier. After this happened, the LORD just began to confirm His will to me by a number of credible prophetic voices outside of our ministry. Five years later, I am writing this book from my assigned place of purpose and destiny.

Many of God's people, instead of living in His Majesty's presence, so that they can ascertain His will for their lives, choose the easier way out. They want a prophet to tell them. So wherever a prophet is ministering, that is where they will go. Instead of going to the prophet to get it second hand, why not go into the Father's presence to get it first hand? When we live in relational fellowship with the Father, the atmosphere of His presence becomes the environment of our spirit. There is a level of faith, confidence, and surety that one walks in, when you have continuous fellowship with the Father. It cannot be manufactured, imitated, or fabricated.

The purpose of sharing these different experiences, is to underscore that God doesn't only deal with you on the spiritual level or concerning spiritual things. He directs the path of our everyday lives. Many Christians relegate God's communication to them only about spiritual things. However, He deals with every area of our lives, even our bad attitudes.

Chapter 8

The Attitude Towards Prayer

*A*ttitude is defined as a settled way of thinking or feeling about someone or something. It is typically reflected in a person's behavior, positioning of the body, expressed in an action or is a mental state. Our attitude or posture toward prayer, will determine whether or not we pray, or how often we pray. I believe that a lack of understanding as to the purpose and power of prayer, has contributed to a life of little or no prayer for many believers.

On an aircraft, there is what is known as the attitude indicator. It keeps the pilot informed of the orientation of the aircraft relative to Earth's horizon. That is, it provides guidance as to how the plane is positioned while in flight, as it make its way or approach to its destination. Remember in our earlier discussion of "what is prayer", we stated that we should approach the Father in a certain state of consciousness. The same message is being underscored here. Our attitude, or mental state, or mindset concerning prayer, will determine our orientation, posture or approach to the Father.

The Intimacy, Purpose and Power of Prayer

When Jesus' disciples asked Him to teach them how to pray. His opening statement in response to their request was, "When you pray... ". He did not say if you pray, but when you pray. The implication here is that He expects us to pray. He wanted them to have the right attitude towards prayer. That attitude being, that it is not a choice for us to pray, it is a necessity that we do pray.

Jesus opened His teaching on prayer with "Our Father". He wanted them to understand that prayer was directional. It has a particular destination, which is the Throne of God. As a result, He wanted them to have the correct perspective. Prayer has the ability to move the hand and heart of God. That is why He said in 2 Chronicles 7:14, that *"If my people, which are called by my name, shall humble themselves, and pray, and seek my face, and turn from their wicked ways; then will I hear from heaven, and will forgive their sin, and will heal their land."*

After teaching the disciples to pray, "Our Father", Jesus then followed it up with "who art in heaven." He wanted to let them know that the Father was in a place of absolute power and absolute authority. In Isaiah 66:1 the LORD says that Heaven is His throne, and the earth is His footstool. The footstool was a designated piece of furniture that was set before the throne. When the king sat on his throne, he would place his feet on his foot stool. In ancient times, when an enemy was subdued, the victor would place his foot on the neck of the defeated enemy. That action was to say that I am greater than you, and you are under my authority.

The feet also speaks of ownership. In Joshua 1:3, the LORD told Joshua that everywhere his feet would tread upon, that it was given to him. Psalm 24:1 says that the earth is the LORD's and the fullness thereof. This is to further establish that the earth is His footstool, or the place that He has ownership of and authority in. In order to establish the right attitude concerning prayer in the hearts of His disciples, Jesus wanted them to know that the one who is their Heavenly Father is in full control of everything.

When He taught them to pray, "give us this day our daily bread", He was teaching them to recognize and understand that the Father was the source of everything, and that they were to look in faith only to Him. When He taught them to pray "forgive us our trespasses", He wanted them to understand that the Heavenly Father was merciful, compassionate, and long suffering. He wanted them to understand that the Father must be approached on the basis of relationship, reverence, and humility.

In Matthew 6:25-33, Jesus tells us to take no thought for our life, what we are going to eat, drink or wear. He said that after all these things do the Gentiles seek. He goes on to assure us that our Heavenly Father knows that we have need of these things. He said to seek first The Kingdom of God, and His righteousness, and all these things will be added unto us. Jesus was letting us know that He did not want any need or lack to interfere with our attitude towards God. Therefore, He told us how to set our priorities and adjust our perspective as we approach Him.

A few years ago, I used to work as a business to business sales representative. I sold digital office solutions. That's just a fancy way of saying that I sold copiers, printers, and other multifunction equipment. I had a $35,000 a month quota. That means that I had to bring in that amount of revenue each month. There were months that I met the quota and other months I did not. If I did not meet the quota of the current month, then the deficit for the current month would have to be made up the following month. That is, the current month's deficit would be added to the quota for the following month.

Sales can sometimes be like the tide. When it comes in, it comes in, but when it goes out, it goes way out. Not every month is a stellar month. As a result of this, sales representatives would sometimes come under a lot of stress. The repercussion of the failure to meet the quota, was possible depression. To generate business, we would do cold calling, which meant soliciting businesses without first having a lead or prior information on the business prospect. At other times we would physically go out and canvas different areas within our assigned territory. This meant trying really hard to "muster up" as much business as possible. After a while, the job became burdensome, monotonous, and boring. All the activity I was doing was not generating any business. I no longer wanted to be there, so I just went through the motions.

I think that many of God's people have this same attitude towards prayer. They see praying everyday as a quota that has to be met, and if they did not pray one day, they feel guilty and depressed. This is because religious Christianity gave us this religious quota that we have to meet every day. Pray, read your bible, fast, etc. After a while, this regiment can become burdensome, laborious, and taxing. So to try to meet this requirement, we end up carrying out a lot of mechanical activities without fruitfulness or productivity. As a result, we feel like we are not getting anywhere. We get depressed and discouraged, and take on a subconscious attitude against prayer, which gives it no gravity or priority in our life.

Some people have made prayer so pseudo deep and spooky, that it makes having a prayer life unattainable. Sometimes also, if we pray for things, and we do not see the satisfying or fulfilling results that we seek, we erroneously conclude that either God did not hear us, or that prayer does not work. We can also become so distracted or sidetracked by other things, that they take precedence in our lives. We then get to the point where we do not realize that in the area of fellowship with the Father, we may be found wanting.

The Intimacy, Purpose and Power of Prayer

Praying begins with the spirit of prayer, and not with the mere act of praying. We have to change our attitude toward prayer if it is to become a lifestyle for us. We don't pray to meet some religious quota. We pray to meet in fellowship with the Father. Getting the God inspired attitude towards prayer, is half the battle. This is how the spirit of prayer works. God will put an appetite and a desire in your heart for Him. That desire and hunger will cause you to yearn and long for Him. This in turn will cause you to seek Him in prayer to satisfy that hunger. However, as we seek to satisfy the initial hunger, our desire for Him will only intensify. Therefore, the fire of desire is never quenched.

Deuteronomy 4:24 says that God is a consuming fire. Every manifestation of God in both Covenants was characterized by fire. So everything that pertains to God has to do with fire. Proverbs 20:27 says that the spirit of man is the lamp of the LORD (NKJV). In the bible days, the wick of the lamp was lit by fire. Fire was the means of light and heat. So when you ask God to release upon you a spirit of prayer, you are in essence asking Him to light the lamp of your spirit with a burning hunger and appetite for Him. Remember that Jesus only taught His disciples to pray after they entreated Him. This is the thing however. Although God will light the lamp of your spirit with the fire of prayer, it is your responsibility to fan the flames of that fire, to keep it burning. Whenever you feel the unction to pray, do not quench it. That is a sure way of extinguishing the fire and putting out the flames, if you keep doing so over a period of time. When we pray under the God inspired spirit of prayer, it takes away the mechanical, just going through the religious motion attitude. It allows us to engage in effectual and fervent prayer.

One of the great things about operating under the spirit of prayer is that, when we find ourselves at a point where we do not know how to pray, or what exactly to pray for, God's Spirit takes over (Romans 8:26). This gives greater and easier access to the Holy Spirit, to help our infirmities, because we know not what to pray as we ought. So remember, prayer has as much to do with attitude, as it does with the rendezvous. So don't try to pray out of religious obligation, because when we do, it becomes more about meeting a quota than about meeting with the King.

The Intimacy, Purpose and Power of Prayer

Chapter 9

Why Should We Pray?

*P*roverbs 4:7, admonishes us to get wisdom, and with all our getting we are to get understanding. In Proverbs 24:3 we are told that *"Through wisdom is an house builded; and by understanding it is established."* Understanding is the illumination and enlightenment received from knowledge or instruction. It enables us to benefit from the imparted knowledge. To establish means to place or position firmly on a fixed, solid, and stable foundation. The thing that has been making our prayer life inconsistent, unstable and unfruitful, is the lack of understanding. Not having the understanding of what you are doing, or why you are doing it, makes the activity that is being undertaken feel like a waste of time. This is the frustration that many of God's people face. Some do not know how to pray. Some do not know what to pray. Others do not know why they should pray. Therefore, their spiritual foundation is unstable.

In Matthew 6:10, Jesus said that we are to pray *"Thy kingdom come, Thy will be done in earth, as it is in heaven."* In teaching His disciples how to pray, He also included in that model, the most important reason why they should pray. One of the purposes of prayer is to call for the establishment of

God's Kingdom in the earth. We are in essence to function as ambassadors of God's kingdom in the earth, who are tending to the business of the King. Jesus was letting us know that the will and purpose of God cannot be done, carried out, executed, or fulfilled without His people praying in the earth.

The concept of kingdom in this context has to do with the rule, will, culture and influence of God in the earth realm. The principle here, is that a king cannot have influence, legislate laws, or exercise his will over a territory that is not a part of his dominion or domain.

The scripture says that Satan is the prince of the power of the air and the god of this world. This was not always the case. Genesis 1: 26-27 tells us that God made man in His own image and gave him dominion and rule in the earth. The word image in Hebrew means a shadow or representation. So when God created man in His image, He actually filled man with a representation of Himself. The earth, therefore, was God's created domain and man was His co-regent.

God's original purpose and intention was to colonize the earth with the culture and values of Heaven. When man fell into sin, because of the devil's deception, he lost his place in the Kingdom. This caused a shift in the balance of power. The supplanter, (the devil), now had the upper hand. This made Jesus' sacrifice on Calvary of great necessity. His sacrifice created the way for us to regain our Kingdom citizenship, thereby reinstating our original position.

When man fell, he also gained the sin consciousness (Genesis 3:22). Sin created a separation between us and the Father. Man no longer enjoyed the comfort of having fellowship with the Father in the cool of the day. In order to survive, man had to toil in order to eat. To reproduce after his own kind, caused pain and suffering. This was not the God kind of life that man was created in. To live in sin, is to live in the sin consciousness or to live according to the flesh. In order to live according to the Spirit, we have to live in the God consciousness. How do we succeed in doing that? We have to get back into continuous fellowship with the Father. Remember, when we approach the Father in prayer, we have to approach Him in the correct state of consciousness, that is, the God consciousness.

The scripture says "For as many of you as have been baptized into Christ have put on Christ" (Galatians 3:27). When we are buried under the water in baptism, this is symbolic of our earth (flesh) experiencing rebirth, as the earth did in the beginning. Sin makes our lives void and empty and full of darkness. When the scripture says that we have put on Christ, it is saying that we have been re-imaged (Romans 8:29). We have been re-instated to our original position in Christ. But now in order to maintain that position, we have to walk in the God consciousness. This is where prayer has its place in our lives. Its purpose is to keep us in fellowship with the Father, thereby restoring our God consciousness.

In Genesis 3, Satan is recorded as having stolen the kingdom from man by deceit. Seeing that he is the god of this world, the earth has now become enemy territory. Therefore, anything that has been released from the heavens to the earth realm, has got to pass through his domain. As a result, he is able to interfere with, intercept, block or delay any message or release that comes from the Kingdom of Light, to the earth. We see evidence of this in Daniel 10:12-13.

Daniel prayed fervently for twenty one days until he was visited by an angel of the LORD, who came for his words. He said from the first day that Daniel began to pray, his prayers were heard, yet it took twenty one days for the angel to get to him. What was happening during that time? The angel said that while he was on his way to Daniel, the prince of the kingdom of Persia intercepted his journey. However, another angel of higher rank, Michael, was dispatched to help him. It was then that he was able to break through enemy lines to get to Daniel. This encounter is a testimony as to the power of our prayers. When we pray, we cause the enemy's resistance to break, thereby creating an opening in the heavens. This allows what God has to release to us, to find its place of manifestation in the earth. Another purpose of our prayers then, is to cause a breach in the enemy's line of defense, so that what God has released can have a clear passage to come through.

It took twenty one days for the angel to fight through the enemy's defense. This means that there will be times when we seem to be waiting forever to get an answer from God. But rest assured, that if we pray according to the will of the Father, the heavens will respond. We just need to have the spiritual stamina to keep praying until a breach is created in the enemy's defenses.

Even though man lost control over his domain, he did not lose his legal rights or claim to it. The control was only illegally or illegitimately transferred from man to the devil. The devil's intent in deceiving man was to have man condemned forever, without any hope of redemption. However, because of his pride and ignorance, the devil could not see that the all-knowing God had a plan to execute in a new place, at a set time. This plan was to have the seed of the woman (Genesis 3:15), who was the Son of God, defeat the devil at the place called Calvary, in the fullness of time (Galatians 4:4). So through this plan, God is able to win back the hearts of all those who would come to Him in faith through Christ. In terms of relationship, we are called sons of God, in terms of fellowship we are called the New Covenant Community of Believers, and in terms of kingdom mandate we are called the ekklesia.

The Intimacy, Purpose and Power of Prayer

In order for redeemed man, or the ekklesia, to now work as an operative for The Kingdom of God, he had to come back into agreement with Heaven, which leads me to Matthew 16:13-19. When Jesus came to the city of Philippi, He asked His disciples as to what people were saying about Him. They responded that some were saying He was one of the prophets or such and such a person. He asked them directly, "who do you say that I am?" Peter spoke up, responding that *"Thou art the Christ, the Son of the living God."* He said unto Peter, " ... *flesh and blood hath not revealed it unto thee, but my Father which is in heaven."* What Jesus was in essence saying to Peter was that you just simply said in agreement, what you heard my Father in Heaven say. Then He said unto Peter "upon the foundation of this revelatory truth, I will build my ekklesia." In verse 19, He tells Peter that He is giving him the keys of the Kingdom of the Heavens. What is significant about this declaration, is that the ekklesia and the Kingdom of the Heavens are inextricably linked and connected by way of the keys and Christ.

The ekklesia was a term that was used to describe the gathering of Greek citizens to deal with the legislative matters and council deliberation of their city state. They were citizens who were concerned with the affairs of their government. The ekklesia represented a political gathering and not a religious one. This word, ekklesia, was translated from its Hebrew counterpart with the same general meaning. By calling this new assembly, the ekklesia, Jesus was establishing the nature and purpose of this entity. Members of the ekklesia are citizens of the Kingdom of The Heavens, according to Philippians 3:20. As citizens, our concern must be with the affairs of our government. Whatever the will and agenda of the host country is, must be what is established in the colony. This goes to the heart of Jesus' narrative. He gave His ekklesia the keys of the kingdom. Keys speaks of authority, the right of access, government, and identity. Keys are mentioned in several places in the scriptures. In Isaiah 22:20-23, we read a prophecy about Eliakim, which is really a prophecy about the reign of Christ. The LORD is saying that He shall dress Christ in royal and kingly attire. He will put the government into His hands, and He will place the keys of David on His shoulders. In his prophecy about Christ, Isaiah 9:6 tells us that *the government shall be upon his shoulder....* In Isaiah 22:22, we are told that the keys will be what is placed on his shoulder. So we see that keys here speaks of governmental authority and the power to permit or forbid.

We also read in Luke 11:52, where Jesus rebukes the Pharisees for withholding the key of knowledge from them who would enter in. So here the key of knowledge speaks of access. We finally read in Revelation 1:18, where Jesus declares that He has the keys of hell and death. In chapter 3:7, He declares that He also has the keys of David. If you noticed, the two passages we read earlier in Isaiah speaks about the government being upon Jesus' shoulder. Now we see Jesus giving the keys of The Kingdom to His ekklesia (just the apostles at the time). The scripture in Ephesians 4, says that we are the Body of Christ, the same passage also said that Christ is the head. My question to you is, where is the shoulder? Is it a part of the head or a part of the body? I believe we all agree that the shoulder is a part of the body, and not a part of the head. When Jesus, therefore, gave the key to His apostolic body, in essence, He was placing the government on His own shoulder. Thus beginning to fulfill the two passages we read in Isaiah 9:22 concerning Himself.

One thing that is important to correctly interpret the scriptures, is its tense, mood, content, and context. Which leads me to my next point. After giving Peter the keys, He said to him that whatsoever you loose on earth, shall be loosed in Heaven, and whatsoever you bind on earth shall be bound in Heaven. Many preachers and Christians interpret Jesus' statement to Peter as Him giving Peter a blank check. It would almost sound like they believe that Peter was being given the absolute power to command Heaven. When we examine the text, and its tense, we will get the clear and correct understanding. The binding and loosing that Jesus spoke about, was a Hebrew idiom or figure of speech. Binding and loosing was a well-known idiom in rabbinic literature, and Jesus was a trained Rabbi. He also knew that His Hebrew disciples would understand that manner of speech. The Rabbi's and spiritual guides of Israel concluded, that in giving the law, Moses was not clear on certain things, and other areas lacked what they considered to be sufficient detail to enable them to walk in full obedience to the law. For example, the law says that no servile work is to be done on the Sabbath. So the question of course would be, "is traveling on the Sabbath a violation of that ordinance?" They concluded that a person can travel on the Sabbath, but they laid out a set distance that can be travelled on the Sabbath, which was two thousand cubits, (less than a mile), 0.57 miles to be exact. So this was the distance that they were loosed or permitted to travel, on the Sabbath. They were bound or forbidden to travel any further beyond that point. So the distance that they travelled was in agreement to the law that was already passed.

So when Jesus said to Peter, that what you loose on earth shall be loosed in Heaven, and what you bind on earth shall be bound in Heaven. This was written in the perfect tense. The Greek perfect tense, speaks of the present state, resultant upon a past action. "Shall be bound in Heaven" is a perfect passive participle. According to this Greek tense, Jesus was telling His apostles, that whatsoever you permit, or declare lawful in the earth, must be what Heaven has already declared to be so. Jesus was letting them know that they took their cue from Heaven, and whatsoever they did, was to be in agreement with Heaven. Heaven is the place of seed, and the earth is the place of harvest. Heaven is the place of decree, and the earth is the place of manifestation. So whatsoever the will and purpose of God is, that has been decreed in the Heavens, God need people in the earth realm to declare/pray those things in agreement with the Heavens, so that His kingdom will come, and His will be done on earth, as it has been decreed in the Heavens.

So this is why Jesus established His ekklesia, and gave us the keys, or the authority to engage kingdom mandates, and execute kingdom protocols. When man fell, and by default surrendered the kingdom to Satan, the lines of communication were severed, and the channels of diplomatic relations were closed. In building His ekklesia, Jesus was letting His chief ambassadors know, that the lines of communication between Heaven and Earth will soon be open, and that diplomatic relations will soon be restored. Prayer is the line of communication between the heavens and the earth realm.

In establishing man, whom He created in His image, and made him His co-regent in the earth, God has established a protocol, that He will not violate or circumvent. So if He is to do anything in the earth, He needs the license of man's prayer of agreement. So prayer is very important to the fulfillment of God's will, purpose, mandate, and agenda. That is why you see in scripture, where God is always "looking for a man." We read in Isaiah 6:8, where the LORD asks, *"Whom shall I send, and who will go for us?"* Isaiah 59:16-17 says, *"And he saw that there was no man, and wondered that there was no intercessor: therefore his arm brought salvation unto him; ...."* In Ezekiel

Why Should We Pray?

22:30, it reads, *"And I sought for a man among them, that should make up the hedge, and stand in the gap before me for the land, that I should not destroy it: but I found none. (v 31) Therefore have I poured out mine indignation upon them; I have consumed them with the fire of my wrath: their own way have I recompensed upon their heads, saith the LORD God."* The LORD asked Himself this rhetorical question in Genesis 18:17, *"... Shall I hide from Abraham that thing which I do"*. As He revealed His intentions to Abraham, Abraham began to pray and intercede for the city.

When we, as the Ekklesia, do not function in our diplomatic capacity, it forces God to do what He does not really want to do. When Mordecai heard, in Esther 4, the pending fate of his people, the Hebrews, he sent word to Esther, who was also a Hebrew, to go in to her husband, the king, and intercede for her people. She informed Mordecai that she had not been called into the presence of the king for thirty days. She also reminded him of the fatal end of anyone who dared to approach the king, when he had not called for them. He then informed her of the fate of herself, and her family, if she failed to use, or pull on the benefit and currency of her relationship with the king. He asked her this thought provoking and heart gripping question, *" ... who knoweth whether thou art come to the kingdom for such a time as this?"* The LORD takes our calling to pray very seriously. It is a matter of spiritual life or the second death to many.

The Intimacy, Purpose and Power of Prayer

In Matthew 21:12-13, the scripture says that "*Jesus went into the temple of God, and cast out all them that sold and bought in the temple, and overthrew the tables of the moneychangers, and the seats of them that sold doves, (v 13) And said unto them, It is written, My house shall be called the house of prayer; but ye have made it a den of thieves.*" This He said in quoting Isaiah 56:7. The context for this setting is this. When Jesus entered into the temple, and saw how the people were being robbed and taken advantage of, He became very incensed. The worshippers who came to the temple, to offer up sacrifice, and celebrate the Passover, especially those who travelled from afar, were being cheated. They had to buy the animal that they used to offer up for sacrifice. In order to do so, they had to make the purchase with temple coins. For that to happen, they had to deal with the people in the temple who would give them a currency exchange. The problem was that the people were being charged an outrageous rate of exchange. In doing this, they were robbing the people.

The other thing was that they had set up their businesses in the Court of the Gentiles. By doing this, they ended up "crowding out" the people who had come to worship. We know this to be true, because verse 14 of Matthew 21 tells us that it was after this incident that the lame and the blind came to Jesus in the temple, and He healed them. By doing what they did, they were blocking the purpose and the will of God from taking place. When we as kingdom citizens do not pray, we are also blocking the will and purpose of God from taking place.

Why Should We Pray?

When the LORD said that my house shall be called a house of prayer for all people (Isaiah 56:7), He was not talking so much about the physical brick and mortar temple, as He was referring to the Body of Christ being the House of Prayer. When He said "Destroy this temple, and in three days I will raise it up" (John 2:19), the scripture makes us aware that the Jews did not understand that He was talking about His body.

In Hebrews 3:6, we are told that we are the corporate House of Christ. In Ephesians 2:20-22 we are told that we are the corporate temple of God. In 1 Corinthians 6:19, we are told that our personal and individual body is the temple of the Holy Spirit. So when Jesus said that my house shall be called the house of prayer for all people, He was talking about a people and not a place. When you or I, as God's house, do not pray, the heart of God is troubled. When we do not fulfill our God ordained purpose of being a House of Prayer, we are thieves and robbers, because we are preventing God's purpose from being fulfilled. When we find other matters and things to do with God's house (our lives), outside of our designated and assigned mandate, we are again thieves and robbers. In 1 Corinthians 6:9-10, Paul tells us that no thieves, along with the other listed misfits, shall inherit the Kingdom of God. Prayer is a mandate, not a choice, suggestion, or mere good idea. That is a part of our reason for being the Ekklesia of God.

The Intimacy, Purpose and Power of Prayer

When Jesus said my house shall be called a house of prayer. It was translated using a Greek tense that communicates the idea of "that is what it has been called, and that is what it shall be for all times." So there will never be a time in God's dealing with man, that our mandate to pray will be rescinded. If we allow ourselves to become too busy with our own pursuits, we will not pray. If we allow ourselves to be distracted by our own agenda, we will not respond to God's life call to pray. We don't have to go to a specific place of prayer, we are the House of Prayer. This does not negate the corporate gathering for the Body of Christ to pray. God wants our life of praying to be like rain, and not like a drought. When we allow the Spirit of God to lead us, we will always sense the call to prayer in our spirit. Let us not be like Queen Vashti.

In Esther 1, we are told of a feast that King Ahasuerus of the Kingdom of the Medes and Persians, had thrown. He invited all of the dignitaries, princes, and rulers of his kingdom, which included one hundred and twenty vassal state or provinces. With pomp and pageantry, he showed them the glory and majesty of his excellent kingdom. At the end of one hundred and sixty days of celebration, he wanted to top it off by showcasing his Queen.

One thing that is important to understand, is that in those days, a king would have a harem of beautiful and exotic women. Many of them were daughters of kings from conquered nations. Out of that harem, he would select the woman who would be his wife and Queen. That is the good fortune in which Vashti had found herself. When the king called for her, she would not go. Esther 1:9 tells us that she was having her own feast for the women, in the royal house, which belonged to the king.

Vashti had a few problems. She forgot who she was. As Queen, being "showed off" by the king was a part of the royal protocol. She forgot where she was. She was in the royal house, which belonged to the king. And finally, she was doing her own thing. The king called her to carry out her purpose, and she would not go. As the narrative goes on to tell us, the king had her removed and replaced. As God's house of prayer, we must remember who we are, whose we are, and where we are. In 1 Peter 2:9, we are told that we are a royal priesthood. The priest was the voice of the people to God. In 1 Corinthians 6:19, we are told that we are not our own, but that we were bought with a price. 2 Corinthians 5:17 tells us that we are in Christ. Colossians 1:3 tells us that we have been delivered from darkness, into the kingdom of His dear Son. Having this knowledge and understanding will enlighten us as to why we need to pray.

Being able to pray in the context of knowing who we are, where we are, and whose we are, has to do with knowing and understanding the heart and mind of God. In 1 Samuel 2:35, God said that He would raise up a faithful priest that will do according to that which is in His heart and in His mind. The

The Intimacy, Purpose and Power of Prayer

LORD told Israel in Jeremiah 3:15 that He will give us shepherds after His own heart. God is concerned with His people coming into oneness, or into agreement with His heart and mind, so much so, that He will only raise up people who have such proclivity. He is so concerned with what's in His heart being made manifest, that He gave us supernatural assistance. We are told in Romans 8:26 that *"the Spirit also helpeth our infirmities: for we know not what we should pray for as we ought: but the Spirit itself maketh intercession for us with groanings which cannot be uttered."* The word *infirmity* in the Greek means "want of strength", "weakness" It speaks of the "inability to produce results." By figurative implication, it means to have area(s) of lack or insufficiency. *"With groanings which cannot be uttered"*, speaks of the passion and desires of the godly heart that is too deep for words. The bible speaks of the deep that is in us, calling to the deep that God is. The type or nature of communication that is necessary for Spirit to spirit conversation or interaction, cannot be facilitated by the flesh. The flesh lacks the strength and ability to produce the kind of God intended results that He calls for. The Greek word for *groaning* is *stenagmós* (pronounced sten-ag-mo's). It means "unutterable gushings of the heart". The helping of our infirmities by the Holy Spirit, is Him communicating our heart to God, and praying the mind of God through us, that our natural mind know not of. Verse 27 states that *"He that searcheth the hearts knoweth what is the mind of the Spirit, because he maketh intercession for the saints according to the will of God."* The Spirit takes our prayers outside of the human realm, and puts it in the Heavenly realm. In other words, it takes it out of our frequency and puts it in the frequency of Heaven.

Romans 8:3 states that, *"For what the law could not do, in that it was weak through the flesh, God sending his own Son in the likeness of sinful flesh, and for sin, condemned sin in the flesh."* So we see here, that even though the law was good, it was rendered ineffective, because of the weakness of the flesh. In like manner, our flesh is rendered weak and ineffective in the Spirit, without the help and strength of the Holy Spirit. Jesus came in the flesh to provide the strength of righteousness that the law needed in order to be effective. The Father sends us the Spirit, to provide us with the strength that we need in order to be effective in the Heavenly realm. So we see that praying involves being led by, or being inspired by the Spirit. Praying with the Spirit is praying with the understanding of the mind and will of God. Praying in the Spirit is allowing the Spirit Himself to pray through us. In order for us to know the mind of God, we have to seek the mind of God. Once we know it, we can then work in agreement with Heaven, and declare the heart and mind of God in the earth, or in the life of a person.

In Job 36:32 (AMP), it states that God covers His hand with lightening and commands it to strike the mark. The word for "strike the mark" comes from a Hebrew word for intercessor/intercession. This term is meant to give the imagery of a person launching or throwing a projectile toward a mark at which he is taking aim. It is the figure of someone directing an attack against an intended target. In Job 37:3 (AMP), it tells us that when God covers His hand with lightening, "*He lets it loose under the whole heaven, And His lightning to the ends of the earth.*"

We are given a look behind the scenes in the Throne room of God in the heavens in Revelation 8:3-5. The narrative tells us that an angel, having a golden censer, was given much incense, that he should offer it with the prayers of all saints upon the golden altar, which was before the throne. The smoke of the incense, which came with the prayers of the saints, ascended up before God out of the angel's hand, and the angel took the censer, and filled it with fire from of the altar, and cast it into the earth: and there were voices, and thunderings, and lightings, and an earthquake. Now, if you have been paying close attention, you would have noticed that what took place in this passage, is the same thing that took place in Job 36:32 (AMP). When we pray, we provide God with a mark or a target in the earth to strike. We can see then, that one of the purposes of prayer is to make intercession, or put ourself in the place of another. When we make intercession before God, we are providing Him with a target to strike. If you want your family to be saved, provide God with that target. If you are in need of deliverance, provide God with that mark, etc.

Why Should We Pray?

We will get no response from heaven, until heaven hears from us. In 2 Chronicles 7:14, God said if His people would pray, He would hear from heaven, forgive our sins, and heal our land. Therefore, our prayer is covenant based. When we pray, we are carrying out our part of the agreement, or upholding our side of the covenant. God's fulfillment of His part of the covenant, is Him hearing from Heaven, and forgiving our sins and healing the land. Breaking a covenant brings a curse (Leviticus 26:14-39). What is a curse? A negative consequence that occurs after an event or action is taken, or lack thereof, to prevent it.

So you can clearly see, that prayer is really earth making the first move or initiating the terms of agreement between heaven and earth. Jesus tells us, in Matthew 26:41 that we are to watch and pray, so that we enter not into temptation. In other words, prayer gives us a sense of vigilance, awareness, and a level of spiritual consciousness. If we look at Leviticus 6:12-13, we will see a prophetic type and shadow of prayer. The LORD told Moses that the fire on the altar of sacrifice must burn continually both day and night, and must never be allowed to be extinguished or go out. He said that the priest must feed it continually with wood, so that the fire go not out. According to 1 Peter 2:9, we are God's priesthood. As the priests of God, we have the responsibility to maintain a consistent, constant, and fervent (hot, heat producing) prayer life. The New Covenant counterpart to this command is in 1

The Intimacy, Purpose and Power of Prayer

Thessalonians 5:17, where Paul tells the Thessalonians to pray without ceasing. The phrase "praying without ceasing" carries the idea of praying with regularity, continuity, or constantly. In other words, he was telling them to make prayer a constant lifestyle practice. In Luke 18:1-8, Jesus shares a parable with His disciples to stress the importance of prayer. He wanted to emphasize the fact that men ought always to pray and not faint, according to the summary or moral of the parable in verse 1.

When we pray, the answer that we receive is based not only on what we pray, but on our capacity to receive. When the widow woman was told by Elisha to go and borrow vessels so that she could receive the miracle of the filling of the oil, the amount of vessels that she had, determined the volume of oil that she received, or the magnitude of her miracle. The scripture says that when they ran out of vessels, the oil stayed (2 Kings 4: 1-7). In other words, it stopped flowing. The time that we spend in the presence of the LORD, and the "amount" of His word that we have in our hearts, will work to increase our capacity for the things that God wants to give to us.

Chapter 10

Draw Near
(Rebuilding the Altar)

The narrative in 1 Kings 18:30 says that after the people came near, Elijah repaired the altar of the LORD that was broken down. A life without prayer, or a life without consistent and effective prayer, is a life with a broken down altar. The word repair means to renew or restore. It carries the idea of rebuilding. After the altar was repaired according to verse 33 of 1 Kings 18, the sacrifice was laid upon it.

In the western paradigm, when we hear of the word sacrifice, we automatically define it as something that we have to give up. For example, we might consider giving up time, money, or pleasure as a sacrifice. We even consider a police officer losing his/her life in the line of duty a sacrifice. The Hebrew concept of sacrifice was not a giving up, but a giving over. It had to do with the permanent transfer of a natural thing to the Devine. As long as sacrifice is defined as giving up something, then pain and loss becomes associated with it. The truth of the matter is that those are two human experiences that we all try hard to run away from. No one wants to feel pain, and certainly no one wants to suffer loss.

The Intimacy, Purpose and Power of Prayer

With the Hebrew concept of transferring over, comes the understanding of transformation. If you notice in Romans 12:1-2, renewal and transformation comes after presenting your body as a living sacrifice. This is in keeping with the scripture that says, "give and it shall be giving to you" (Luke 6:38). If we view sacrifice correctly, as giving over something to God, as opposed to giving up something, then we will be reminded that God will not leave a void or empty place in us. When we give over to God, He will give back something to replace it.

The word for sacrifice in Hebrew is *korban*. It is derived from the word that means "to come near, or to approach". What is significant about the sacrifice, is that it is one of the many offerings that has to do with food. For example, there is the grain offering, sin offering, burnt offering, and guilt offering. You may ask "why does the Devine need food?" In ancient times, food was an integral and central part of the culture. It was the means of fellowshipping, exhibiting closeness, friendship and intimacy. It was shared between people of relational commonality. That is why the LORD commanded Israel not to eat meat or food offered to idols. It was being offered to demons.

The scripture says that if we draw nigh to God, He will draw nigh to us (James 4:8). To draw near, by implication, means to come closer. In Hebrew, it means "approach to offer". Paul also said in his epistle that if a brother is known to be a fornicator,

Draw Near (Rebuilding the Altar)

not to eat with such a person. Since sharing of food was an expression of friendship, closeness and fellowship, it was important not to eat with such a person, or eat food offered to idols. This would mean that we are partaking of the same lifestyle or drawing near to idols.

One of the reasons why the LORD required sacrifice in some form of food, was because it was the connection of fellowship, friendship, and intimacy between Himself and Israel, that He wanted to establish in their hearts and minds. That is why Jesus used the allegory, *"He that eateth my flesh, and drinketh my blood, dwelleth in me, and I in him."* He was speaking of Himself as the "bread of life" (flesh) or the "sacrificial lamb" that shed His blood, in giving Himself as a sacrifice for us. This is why Ephesians 2:13 states that we who were afar off, have been made nigh or near, by the blood (sacrifice) of Christ.

The Intimacy, Purpose and Power of Prayer

Chapter 11

What is the Altar in the Life of a Believer?

*I*f our body is the temple of the LORD, that makes our heart His altar. As a result, the heart/altar is a very sacred place. That is why God will not accept sacrifices from a corrupt or profane altar/heart. He will not accept a heart that holds jealousy, hatred, bitterness, unforgiveness, or any kind of offense. If we offer sacrifice with a heart that is in such a condition, then our heart becomes the altar of devils, and those meats, (the issues in our hearts), becomes a sacrifice unto them. We then become guilty of idol worship. Those idols we are told of in Deuteronomy 32:17, are devils. As a result, our heart becomes a den of thieves, who are allowed to use the LORD's temple for their own plans and purposes, according to Matthew 21:13.

The altar is the unity of prayer with an engaged heart. It is the place from which connection is made. It is the place from where love, compassion and goodness are issued. The altar is the seat of all that we are. That is, it involves our whole heart, mind and soul. It is the place of giving and receiving.

The Intimacy, Purpose and Power of Prayer

(i) The altar testifies to the recognition of the existence of the god you believe in. Whether it be the one true God, or an idol that is worshipped as God. To not have an altar to a god, is to testify against their existence.

(ii) An abandoned or broken down altar speaks of a god that was once believed in, or worshipped as a god, but is no longer recognized or acknowledged as such. If you or I had lived in ancient times, we would have seen a lot of altars of the sort that is spoken of in 1 Kings 18:30.

(iii) Your altar is your god's legitimacy, and your sacrifice is your voice. In Hebrews 11:4, we are told that even though Abel was dead, by his sacrifice, he still spoke. Those who have no altar, have no sacrifice, and those who have no sacrifice, have no voice.

(iv) Whenever God sends a word or a blessing, He always direct it to a specific place. When Elijah was sent to Zarephath, he became the word and blessing for the widow there. When Elisha was sent to the barren woman's house, he stirred up her spirit to build him a room, so that he could stay there when he was passing through. He released her word and blessing that he was carrying. This manifested as a fertile womb, thereby causing her to bare a man child. Your altar and sacrifice provides Heaven with an address or zip-code to which your word, your blessing, or your breakthrough will be sent.

(v) Our altar is the foundation of our connection and relationship with the Father. It is the channel and communication highway between heaven and earth. It is the ladder that allows the spirit of man to ascend into His presence, and to allow His presence to descend, to accept the sacrifice of man that is offered up.

(vi) In connecting to His presence, the first thing to be built is the altar. However, if at any time that altar was abandoned, reconnecting to His presence requires that the altar be rebuilt (Revelation 2:5). God wants a personal connection for corporate impact, which will lead to personal effect in the kingdom or global influence. This means our corporate impact is only as strong as our personal connection to the LORD. This personal connection leads to our personal effect in the Kingdom. Together, each of our personal effect, becomes a global influence.

To have an altar and no sacrifice, is to be like the fig tree that had blossomed, but when approached for fruit, there was none. Before we can expect to experience the supernatural workings of God in our lives, or see the manifestations of His

Glory, we must first come near, repair the altar, and prepare the sacrifice.

In the narrative of the Holy Script, there are at least three distinct occasions where we read that God's glory was brought down.

(i) When the specific dwelling places that God gave detailed instructions to build, were established.

(ii) When Elijah repaired the altar.

(iii) When Moses was called up to the mount of Sinai.

The glory appeared at the completion of the Tabernacle of Moses and the Temple of Solomon. The bible tells us that we are both the temple and the sacrifice. To be a temple without an altar and a sacrifice, is to be a temple without the glory or the Fire Presence of the LORD.

What is the Altar in the Life of a Believer?

For your personal study: How do I rebuild my altar? How do I prepare my sacrifice? I am so glad that you asked. Begin by studying 2 Chronicles 7:14, Matthew 6:33 and Revelation 2:5.

Chapter 12

We are an Offering

When, or for whatever reason, we neglect to position ourselves as a living sacrifice to God, we are refusing to draw near to Him. We are refusing to make any kind of intimate or relational connection with Him. Communion and fellowship in prayer, is how we posture ourselves as a living sacrifice to God. In not doing that, we are refusing to share a meal with Him. Whether it is on purpose or by default, we are in essence saying to Him, that we have nothing in common.

In Romans 12:1, Paul says *"I beseech you therefore, brethren, by the mercies of God, that ye present your bodies a living sacrifice, holy, acceptable unto God, which is your reasonable service."* We are considered an offering to the LORD. Ephesians 5:26 confirms this as Jesus described how a man should love his wife as Christ loved the church. The scripture continues to say that Christ gave himself for the church so that he might sanctify and cleanse it with the washing of water by the word. This He did so that He might present it to Himself a glorious church, not having spot, or wrinkle, or any such thing, but that it should be holy and without blemish.

When an animal was brought for sacrifice, it could not have any imperfections. The priest had to wash it with water before burning it on the altar. Ephesians said that we are cleansed by the washing of water by the word. This should emphasize to us the importance of the Word of God. The inward part of the sacrifice and its legs were washed. The washing of our inward parts by the word, is carried out by us hiding the word in our hearts, so that we do not sin against God (Psalm 119:11). When we do not sin, we do not incur any blemish or imperfections on our sacrifice.

In order for us to hide the word in our hearts, we have to study the word. When we study the word, it will cause us to pray fervent, effectual prayers. As we discussed earlier, these kind of prayers will yield the intended results, if we dwell in righteousness. The word sin in Hebrew means to miss the mark. Therefore, without the word in us to make an indelible impact in our prayers, we will miss the mark, or sin against God, and thereby not get the desired result.

Deuteronomy 4:24 and Hebrews 12:29 says that our God is a consuming fire. Leviticus 1:9 says that the *"priest shall burn all on the altar, to be a burnt sacrifice, an offering made by fire, of a sweet savor unto the LORD."* This tells us that when the offering was made, it gave off a pleasant aroma that was pleasing to the LORD. So it is, that when we present ourselves to the Holy One in prayer, as a holy and acceptable living sacrifice, (having been washed with word on the inside), that the consuming fire, that is God, will consume our offering, so that the sweet savor of our prayers will rise before Him.

If you read in Genesis about the life of Abraham, you will find that his life was characterized as an altar builder. Everywhere that he went, he built an altar to offer up sacrifice unto the LORD. Our altar is our prayer life, which in turn becomes the table of the LORD. Our body/life then becomes our fellowship meal sacrifice. When Paul said that we are to present our body as a living sacrifice, he is speaking in contrast to the Old Testament Sacrificial System, wherein a dead sacrifice was offered upon the altar. He made no specific mention of an altar, because it was the logical conclusion, that if a sacrifice is spoken of, then an altar is suggested or implied.

When a person brought their sacrifice to the priest, once it was placed upon the altar, a transfer or "turn over to", took place. The gift, or offering, then no longer belonged to the giver, but to the receiver, or to the LORD. The implication of Paul's directive is to surrender, or turn over self-ownership to God. When we refuse to do this, whether by ignorance or disobedience, we are guilty of stealing what belongs to another, or robbing God.

The Intimacy, Purpose and Power of Prayer

In 1 Corinthians 6:13, the scripture states that our body is for the LORD and the LORD for the body. It goes on to tell us in verses 19-20 that our body is the temple of the Holy Spirit. The altar was a permanent fixture in the temple of God, in the Old Covenant. As it was in the Old covenant temple of brick and mortar, so it is in the New Covenant temple of flesh and blood. When we refuse God what is rightfully His, all we leave Him with is nothing more than an unfulfilled out of body experience. This makes us guilty of breaking the first and the ninth commandments, which are respectively, "you shall have no other god before me" and "thou shall not steal".

The difference between an offering and a sacrifice is this. An offering is giving from what you have, a sacrifice is giving of yourself. The problem with many Christians is that they always try to offer up an offering in place of a sacrifice. That is why they find it easier to offer up their money, their service, or their substance to the church, without really ever giving of themselves as a living sacrifice to God. You do not need an altar to give an offering, but you cannot give a sacrifice without an altar. Let us examine some truths concerning the altar.

Chapter 13

I AM Calling for You Will You Pitch a Tent for Me?

*I*n Exodus 33:7-11, we are told that Moses would take a tent and pitch it outside the camp, some distance away, which was called the tent of meeting. Anyone who wanted to seek God, or enquire of the LORD, would go to the tent of meeting outside the camp. In Deuteronomy 31:14-15, God called Moses and Joshua to present themselves before Him. The word present in Hebrew is *yatsab* (pronounced yaw-tsab). It means to set or station oneself; take one's stand. The Greek word for *present* is *parecho* (pronounced par-ekh-o). It comes from two Greek words. The first word is *para*, which means "from close beside" and *exo* "have." So the word present means to have close beside, "to give in an up close and personal" manner. That is what Paul meant in Romans 12:1, when he said that we are to present our bodies a living sacrifice to God. We are to come close, and offer ourselves as a sacrifice.

The Intimacy, Purpose and Power of Prayer

The LORD called this meeting with Moses and Joshua because he wanted to make preparations for the children of Israel after Moses' death. There are several other places in the Holy Script where people were called to present themselves before the LORD. Some of these scriptures include:

(i)   Exodus 23:14-17

We are told that there were three times a year that all the men in Israel were to appear before the LORD. These times were the Feast of Unleavened Bread, the Feast of Harvest, and the Feast of Ingathering, also known as Passover, Pentecost, and Tabernacles respectively. These were set times that the Sovereign LORD had ordained. They were instructed to not come before Him empty, but to bring a gift or an offering. When we go before the LORD, we must not go empty. We must go filled with praise, worship, thanksgiving, faith, expectation and reverence.

(ii)   Numbers 11:16-25

In this scripture, we see the result of Moses' complaint to God, that it was too great a burden to lead the people by himself. God then instructed Moses to select seventy elders from among the people whom he knew to be men of character and integrity, and bring them before the tabernacle of the congregation.

I AM Calling for You
Will You Pitch a Tent for Me?

(iii)   Exodus 24:9-18

In this scripture God called Moses to come up to the mount to meet with Him, that He may give him the tables of stone with the law and commandments engraved on them.

From these examples, we can clearly see that being called before the LORD by God Himself, was a regular practice by His Majesty.

We can choose to remain in our comfort zone, or choose to remain in our place of familiarity, and be satisfied with the status quo, the accepted norm, or the ordinary. Or we can present ourselves at the "tent of meeting", so we can hear what God is saying, know what God is doing, and see where God is going.

God was about to separate Moses and Joshua through death. When God calls you to the tent of meeting, to meet with Him, it is because there are some things that He wants to bring to an end and closure in your life. In this narrative, Moses and Joshua were two separate individuals. Prophetically, Moses and Joshua together represents you the individual. God wants to separate you from where you are coming from, and connect you to where you are going. Moses symbolically represents what God had done. Joshua represents what God has purposed to do. Moses represents what had been. Joshua represents what is coming, or soon to be. Moses spoke of where God is coming from and Joshua speaks to where God is going next. Moses was now coming to the end of his season, while Joshua was getting ready to enter into the beginning of his. This was to mark the end of Joshua's season with Moses.

Where you are coming from cannot enter in with you to where you are going. You represent both what God has done in you, and what He has purposed to do in you. You represent both where God has taken you from, and where He is taking you to. He has to speak between the two seasons of you. The word that brings closure to one season in your life, is the same word that will usher you into the next season of your life. To present yourself before Him, is to grant Him access to speak, or declare His will/words to you.

According to ancient royal protocol, you did not just appear in the courts of the king without being called or summoned. If you had the audacity to break with protocol, and the king did not extend his scepter to you, you would be executed. Execution was ordered on the spot without mercy. This was the concern that Queen Esther voiced to Mordecai (Esther 5:1-3), seeing that she had not been called into the presence of the king for the past thirty days. As a result of our covenant positioning in Christ, we do not have to have that same fear when we present ourselves before the LORD. Why? Because He has given us uncommon access.

I AM Calling for You
Will You Pitch a Tent for Me?

When Jesus died on the cross, the account in scripture tells us that the veil in the temple tore in two (Matthew 27:51). This was symbolic of open access for us to enter freely into the throne room of the King. So since we have been given this access, the scripture says that we should go boldly to the Throne of Grace. This means that we can take full advantage of presenting ourselves before the LORD in prayer at any time, because He is always available to us. We do not have to fear. We do not have to wait for Him to call us. We can just go boldly.

As is evident in the Old Testament scripture (Deuteronomy 31:14-15), it was a regular occurrence for Moses to go into the presence of the LORD. In this instance however, the LORD called for both him and Joshua to present themselves before Him. He gave this summons as it pertained to His purpose and intentions toward them. The Father has told me to tell you, that He is calling you to present yourself in the tent of meeting before Him. All because of His purpose and intentions concerning you and your season. He has told me to tell you that your appearance before Him cannot be mechanical or religious. You have to present yourself in a very close and personal way.

You will know when God is calling you to the tent of meeting when He calls you to a time or season of fasting and prayer. You will know when He is calling you to the tent of meeting, when He wakes you up to pray at a different time from your regular time of prayer, for a season.

The Intimacy, Purpose and Power of Prayer

Spending time in the tent of meeting with Him will provide us with the strength level, endurance level, and "wisdom keys" that we need to carry out His agenda and purpose. The LORD said in Zechariah 4:6 "that it is not by might, nor by power, but by my Spirit". So if you want to remain on the "cutting edge" of your walk and relationship with the Father, you need to be like Joshua in Exodus 33:11. This scripture tells us that Joshua remained in the tent even after Moses ended speaking with God, and returned to the camp. The LORD did not ask Joshua to stay behind. Joshua remained in the tent because he wanted an experience with God for himself. He stayed of his own will. Will you stay in the presence of God long enough that you won't want to leave? Joshua's love, hunger, passion, and his longing for God asked him to stay in God's presence. What is your love, hunger, passion, and longing, asking you for, or asking you to do?

In Exodus 33, Moses asked God for His presence to go with them to the "Promised Land", and for God to show him His Glory. What are you asking God for? Are you asking for houses, land, finances, etc? Are you asking for things that pertain to you? God said to Moses, "there is a place by me......". The place by God, that He is calling us to, is the tent of meeting.

You may ask "what is the tent of meeting?" or "where is this tent of meeting located?" The tent of meeting was also called the Tabernacle of the Congregation. As stated earlier, it was pitched outside the camp, and the Children of Israel resorted there to seek the LORD. This was a literal camp. What is the camp in your life that you have to leave out of to get to your tent of meeting? He wants us to pitch Him a tent outside of our busy life camp. He wants us to pitch it outside of the camp of the hustling of our fast paced and overbooked schedules. He wants us to pitch it outside of the camp of personal or corporate carnality. We should pitch it outside of the camp of mechanic religiosity. We should pitch it outside the camp of societal norms and distractions. The building materials for pitching the tent of meeting are a life of intimate and personal prayer. This involves speaking to, and having intimate, regular, and ongoing fellowship and communion with the Father. It involves living a clean and consecrated life. Jesus said in Matthew 6:6 "when you pray", the very use of the word *"when"* instead of *"If"*, takes it out of the realm of suggestive ambiguity or personal preference. It, therefore, communicates to us that Jesus expects us to pray.

There are a lot of benefits in pitching a tent for the Father. I will just list a few.

(i) It pressurizes the cabin of your spirit.

The reason why the pressure on the outside of a plane

is unable to crush it, is because the pressure on the inside, is of equal strength, or pressure, as on the outside. It is like two men of equal strength arm wrestling. One is not able to put down the arm of the other, thus wining the match, because they are of equal strength. So when we spend time in the tent of meeting with the Father, it helps to strengthen the inner man, and give us internal spiritual fortitude, so that the pressure of life does not weigh us down or crush us, that we collapse in on ourselves.

(ii) When we spend relationship time in His presence, His strength becomes our strength. It is what my spiritual father and mentor, Bishop Roberts, calls "the time of divine transfer." It maintains unbroken fellowship with the Father, and builds up one's faith and confidence in Him and in yourself. We should never take such a long time to go into the LORD's presence, that when we finally go, we feel like a stranger.

I read a story about a competition between two lumberjacks. One was an old man, and his opponent was about twenty years younger than him. They were the last two finalists in the competition. The younger lumberjack was certain that he was going to win. Being stronger and having more endurance, he was sure that the competition was his for the taking. The story goes on to say, that they were both assigned their area to begin competing against each other. The younger lumberjack began very fast like a race horse out of the gate, and maintained a high rate of speed right throughout the competition. He did not stop to rehydrate himself or to rest. He noticed that at different times, the older lumberjack would stop for a period of time, and then start up again. He was certain that each time the older lumberjack stopped he was losing valuable time. He therefore, concluded that since he did not stop to rest or get water, he was ahead of the game. Finally the competition was over, and it was time to name the winner. The young man took his place on the podium, expecting to be declared the winner. To his surprise however, the competition went to the older man, who was declared the winner. Stunned and bewildered, the younger lumberjack asked, "how is it possible for you to win when you stopped to rest so many times." The older lumberjack's response was "that is where you are wrong son." "I did not stop to rest, I stopped at the different times that I did, to sharpen my blade (Reynolds, P.)."

The fact that the younger fellow did not stop at any time to sharpen his blade, meant that he had to work twice as hard, and exert more energy to cut down the trees with a duller axe. When we spend time in the tent of meeting in God's presence, it will sharpen the edge of the blade of our spirit. It will make us more spiritually conscious, more intuitive, and become sharpened in the spirit of discernment. If we behave like the young lumberjack, and just keep depending on our own strength, or our own ability, or our own knowledge, we will not have the endurance or the wisdom to win.

Abraham Lincoln was quoted as saying "give me six hours to chop down a tree and I will spend the first hour sharpening the axe (Reynolds, P.)."

Chapter 14

How Do I Enter Into The Tabernacle of His Presence?

*I*n order to answer the above question, let us refer to the Tabernacle of Moses. The Tabernacle of Moses contained prophetic truths as to how to enter into God's presence. The key thing that must be understood about entering into His presence, is that the fear of the LORD must be the all abiding factor in our lives. The word in Hebrew for this realization is *yirah* (pronounced yir-aw'). It denotes reverence and awe (Psalm 33:6-9, Jeremiah 5:22), hatred of evil (Proverbs 8:13) and obedience to God (Exodus 19:5). The reason why God appeared to the Children of Israel with thunder, lightning, fire, and thick clouds of darkness, was so they may get a sense of the great, terrible, and overwhelming power and might of His presence, and fear Him. To fear the LORD is more than just religious piety, or a mere sense of respect. It involves embracing Elohim's attitude against sin, and to have a deep and profound reverence for His character, integrity, and holiness. The fear of the LORD is a continual humble, and faithful submission to Yahweh. It is meant to be the central compass of a believer's life.

Before the high priest could enter the Most Holy Place, he first had to stop in the outer court to slay the sacrifice, wash at the brazen lava, and change his garment. He would then proceed to the inner court, where he would change the oil in the lamp, change the shewbread, and fill the censer with coals of fire from off the altar of incense. He would then proceed behind the veil, into the most Holy Place, to appear before the LORD. Aaron and his sons would minister in the other two courts, but only the high priest was allowed to go behind the veil. It was only big enough to accommodate two entities, the high priest, and the Ark of the Covenant.

It was never God's intention to select one tribe, or one family to minister before Him. In Exodus 19:5-6, God told Israel that if they would walk before Him, He would make them a peculiar treasure, a kingdom of priests, and a holy nation. As a result of their rebellion and disobedience, He selected the tribe of Levi, to represent the whole nation, in ministering before Him. The Tabernacle of Moses, and the Levitical order, was the system of worship that God had set up as the protocol of approach into His presence. When Jesus came as the Lamb of God to be our savior, He was also in the role of our high priest, according to Hebrews 4:14-16. One difference, was that Christ's priesthood was not after the Levitical order. His priesthood was after the order of

How Do I Enter Into The Tabernacle of His Presence?

Melchizedek. Christ's priesthood was greater than the Levitical priesthood.

Abraham is the father, or patriarch of the House of Israel. The writer of Hebrews 7:4-17 points out, that Melchizedek was so great, that Abraham paid tithes to him. In Genesis 14:18-20, we are told that Melchizedek was the priest of the Most High God, who blessed Abraham. In Hebrews 7:9-10, the writer states explicitly that Levi, who collects the tithes from Israel, paid tithes while he was yet in Abraham's loins. For Levi, was yet in the loins of his father, when Melchizedek met him. The author also tells us that the lesser was blessed of the greater. Seeing, therefore, it has been established that Melchizedek was the priest of God, Abraham and Levi paid tithes to him, the lesser was blessed of the better, and that Christ's priesthood is after the Order of Melchizedek, this then establishes the unequivocal and incontrovertible truth, that Christ's priesthood is greater than the Levitical priesthood, which makes the New Covenant a greater covenant.

In verse 12, of Hebrews 7, the author of Hebrews stated, that seeing there was a change in the priesthood, there also needed to be a change of the law. In the Tabernacle of Moses, only the high priest could go behind the veil into the Presence of the LORD, and only he was allowed to offer up sacrifice, which was done only once per year. Going into the presence of LORD at that time, was characterized by fear. In Exodus 28:1-2, Moses was told to separate Aaron and his four sons, to minister unto the LORD, in the office of the priest. Holy garments were to be made for them, for beauty and for glory.

As stated above, Christ is a high priest of the Melchizedek order. So if Christ is a high priest, where is His priesthood? In 1 Peter 2:9, we are told that we are a royal priesthood, a holy nation, and a peculiar people..... In this new priesthood order, the whole nation of New Covenant Believers are all individual priests of a royal order. According to Hebrews 4:16, we can all come boldly, without fear, to the Throne of Grace, to receive grace and mercy, instead of judgment. We all have unlimited, undeniable and unrestricted access to the Father. As such, we can all offer up sacrifices to God. Our sacrifices are not heifers, sheep, oxen, etc. Our sacrifices are that of praise, thanksgiving, worship, giving, etc. In Hebrews, when the author said that there is a change of the priesthood, what he was really saying, was that the priesthood had evolved to the higher order of the reality, in the heavenly tabernacle. He said that the Aaronic priesthood ministered from the earthly tabernacle, but Christ ministers from the Heavenly tabernacle. That is exactly what Jesus meant when He said to the Samaritan woman, that *"the hour cometh, when ye shall neither in this mountain, nor yet at Jerusalem, worship the Father."* He went on to say, *"But the hour cometh, and now is, when the true worshippers shall worship the Father in spirit and in truth … ."* (John 4:21,23). The implication of what He was saying was that the worship of the Father would no longer be done through types, shadows, or ceremony. It would no longer be through earthly or temporal means. It would now take on the true reality of the heavens. Each time that we read of the prophets being given a vision of heaven, it was never sacrifices of bulls and heifers, but of worship, thanksgiving and praise. That is what Jesus meant when He said, they that worship the Father, must worship Him in the spirit and truth, (of the heavenly reality).

Christ also continued to say that *"God is a Spirit: and they that worship him must worship him in spirit and in truth."* (John 4:24). "In spirit" has nothing to do with speaking in tongues, it has to do with the change from the earthly location, to the Heavenly one.

One thing that has not changed, in all the various changes of the priesthood, is the protocol of approach, or how to enter God's Presence. It is very important for us to understand that falling down on our knees, or laying prostrate on the floor in prayer, does not automatically, or immediately put us in the Father's presence. The first order of protocol, is to put on our priestly garments, for beauty and glory, before entering into the Tabernacle of His presence, thereby, standing in the office of our priesthood. The garments for beauty and glory are put on when we step into our priesthood consciousness.

Many Christians say that they pray to God, but have a hard time praying for various reasons. Some of these reasons are that they find it tedious or boring. Many, many, many

The Intimacy, Purpose and Power of Prayer

Christians, as a result of their religious upbringing, see praying as having a quota that should be met daily. That used to be my experience and testimony for a great part of my Christian life. As a result, we see ourselves as a salesperson who have to make a sales pitch, in trying to sell God on why He needs to answer our prayers. Or we see ourselves as a lawyer, who have to put together a convincing argument, in order to persuade God as to why He should rule in our favor. Some of us even see ourselves as this pitiful and sinful wretch, and a "nobody", who is trying to solicit mercy and pardon, from this dreadful, but gracious God.

Religion has erroneously taught us that this is a sign of humility, and humbleness of heart. As a result, we have developed a sense of self-righteousness, and a sense of loathing for those who do not share this perspective. The truth of the matter is, we have been going before the Father with the wrong mindset. Our mindset determines our consciousness, and our consciousness determines our actions. God has determined the mindset, or consciousness, in which we should approach Him, or enter into the Tabernacle of His presence.

That becomes our key of access. Possessing a key gives access, or a means of entry. Attempting to enter the Tabernacle of God's Presence with the wrong mindset, is like trying to unlock a door with the wrong key. Illegal or violated access calls for expulsion, because it is an offense to the presence of God.

How Do I Enter Into The Tabernacle of His Presence?

Anything that offends God, is cast out of His presence. We see evidence of this when Adam and Eve were cast out of the Eden of God's presence. We also see this in Matthew 22:11-13, when a man was found at the wedding feast of a king's son, without the proper garment on. As a result, the king had him thrown out. This may seem harsh, but it was the cultural custom of the day. If a rich man threw a feast, he would send special garments to all the guests who were invited. If you were not sent a garment, it meant that you were not invited, which in turn meant that you had no legal right to be there. This gave the servants the authority to put you out, or to deny you access.

We, as the Community of New Covenant Believers, have been given the invitation to go boldly to the Throne of Grace. With this invitation, comes the special garments which are required to enter in. God gave the Aaronic Priests garments for beauty and for glory, or as the NIV translation puts it, for honor and dignity. In Isaiah 61:10, we are told that He has also given us, or put on us, the garments of salvation, and the robe of righteousness. We are told in Galatians 3:27, that when we baptize into Christ, we have put on Christ. In Romans 13:14, Paul tells us to be clothed with Christ. The implication being that Christ is our garment. In Ephesians 6:11, we are told to put on the whole armor of God, including the helmet of salvation (verse 17). In Philippians, we are told to let this mind be in us as was in Christ Jesus. The mind of Christ, and helmet of salvation is our mitre, or headdress, which speaks of mindset and consciousness. So when we go to the Throne of Grace, we go in the mindset and consciousness of our new priesthood status and identity. This is the source or origin of our boldness. When we go in that mindset and consciousness, we are appearing in our priestly garments, and the special clothing that was sent to us, due to the nature of our invitation. The bible speaks of our righteousness as filthy rags. To not go in our priestly garments, is to appear before Him in filthy rags. This would cause us to be denied access into His presence, because that is not the garments that He sent to us.

In Matthew 16:19, Jesus told Peter that he was given the keys of the kingdom. In Revelation 3:7, He said that He has the key of David. He said that He opens, and no man can shut, He shut, and no man can open. Those terms respectively means access granted or access denied. Our mindset and consciousness, which speaks of our status and identity in respect to who we are in Christ, is the key of our authority that gives us legal access into His presence.

The priest in the old covenant began his journey into the Tabernacle of God's presence from the outer court. They did not begin from behind the veil. There were duties to be carried out in each court before going behind the veil. The outer court was where they slew the sacrifice, which was to be offered up to God. After offering up the sacrifice, they would wash at the brazen lava before advancing to the inner court. These were necessary steps before going behind the veil.

How Do I Enter Into The Tabernacle of His Presence?

It is important for us to understand that as priests of His presence, it is our priestly duty to minister before Him. It is also imperative for us to understand that worship is the journey into His presence. It is the protocol of kings. In Revelation we are told that we are kings and priests unto Him. Many times we pray, and it feels like our prayer is not getting anywhere, and that God is not hearing us. We may also feel like our prayers are dry, repetitive, or unproductive. The problem is that we are trying to talk to Him from the outer court of our carnality and human experiences.

The outer court is where we slay the flesh, not talk to God. It is the place where we offer up the sacrifice of confession of sins and repentance from sin. We must then move into the inner court of our soul. This is the place where our emotions, feelings, logic, and human reasoning hold rule. It is the place where turbulence and unrest reigns. This where our human experiences work its way into our spirit. This is where illumination and change takes place, if we have sacrificed self from the outer court. This is where the shewbread of life can feed a hungry and thirsty soul. It is in this court that we complete the putting on of our priestly garments.

The robe of righteousness is in approaching His Majesty in faith, and the garment of salvation is approaching Him in the conscious reality and acceptance of our redemption. Once we enter into the inner court of our soul, we can then break bread. Breaking bread in scripture speaks of fellowship. Through this fellowship, illumination, revelation, insight and clarity will be experienced. The garment of praise is extolling Him in recognition of what He has done and is able to do. We must then move from here into the innermost court of our spirit. It is here where the innermost court of our spirit, connects with the innermost court of His Presence. Our regenerated spirit is now connected with eternity. It is the place of further illumination and revelation.

Proverbs tells us that the spirit of the redeemed becomes the realm of the Spirit of God. The Presence of God becomes the realm, the secret place, the sanctuary, or dwelling place of man's spirit. This is where the atmosphere of the Father's presence becomes the environment of our spirit. When in the innermost court of the Father's presence, the desire of His priest will begin to intimately pull on His Spirit. The energy of His Spirit becomes His intimate presence with us. In this innermost place of our spirit and the innermost place of His presence, it is just you and His Majesty. This will be a moment of intimate consummation and "divine exchange." It is at this time that you can let your request be made known unto the Father.

It is important to remember that we cannot talk to the Father from the outer court of our flesh. We have to make the journey to go behind the veil. When you enter behind the veil, you enter into the secret place of the Most High. It is here that the Father feeds your spirit with hidden manna, and reveal secret things to your spirit (Psalm 25:14).

The word *secret* indicates a confidential and intimate dialogue between friends. It is here where the awareness of your spirit will awaken to the awesome brilliance of Him, whom your soul loves, and He, who is the lover of your soul. It is here that your thirsty soul can drink from the refreshing reservoir of His Spirit, and inhale, and absorb the intoxicating breath of His Presence. If your aim is just to pray and tell God what you want, then at the conclusion, you may feel religiously justified. However, if you are driven out of a hunger, longing and deep yearning for His presence, then in His presence you will find fullness of joy, pleasures forever more, and the paths of life. "Oh what fellowship divine!!" It is at this point that we can really, truly, fruitfully, and effectively carry out our priestly duty, and minister to the Father. You will leave from there with the unquestionable conviction and heartfelt assurance, that you are His and He truly is yours.

The Intimacy, Purpose and Power of Prayer

Chapter 15

How Do I Know
When I am in His Presence?

*Y*ou may say, *"Well, what I have read so far all sounds kinda good. But how do I know when I'm in His presence?"* How do you know when you have entered into the Holy of Holies or have actually gone behind the veil? Let me take a step back for a moment. When entering into the Tabernacle of His Presence, you must know why you are going there. God is a God of purpose and intentionality, and this is how we must be as well, when going into His presence. When we enter into the Tabernacle of His Presence, if it is for intimacy (fellowship and communion), then the tabernacle becomes a bedchamber. If it is for counsel or judgment, the tabernacle becomes the Throne room. If it is for strategy or to prepare for battle, the tabernacle becomes the war room. Get acquainted with all the rooms of the Father's house, because the room that you enter, will tell why you are there.

My Journey into His Presence

The first protocol of His Presence is to enter into His gates with thanksgiving and into His courts with praise (Psalm 100:4). When I enter into the Tabernacle of His Presence, I know why I am there, so I begin to engage in praise and worship that fits the occasion of my visit. My praise and worship is offered up based upon who He is. Even though I go into the Father's presence with a particular intent, as I praise and worship Him, my spirit still feels after what direction He wants to go in. I base our time of fellowship upon what He wants to do, because it is His presence that I am in, so I allow Him to take the lead.

I may go there with a request, petition or a need on my heart, but as I am worshipping, I sometimes sense that He wants to have fellowship and communion, so I head for the bedchamber of His presence. In that place, I don't talk about bills or needs I just talk about Him. I tell Him how compassionate and merciful He is. I tell Him how much I love Him, and how much His presence really means to me. I tell Him how faithful and longsuffering He is. I tell Him how that my giving Him praise and worship is much more important to me, than my needs. Sometimes while I am doing that, my spirit just automatically breaks out into singing. I would ask Him what song He would like to hear me sing to Him. There are times that He would raise a song in my spirit, and it would be a song that I had forgotten about, or was not thinking about at the time. That is how I have come to learn His method of selecting a song that He wants to hear. As I continue to follow His lead, my spirit begins to lose a sense of time consciousness. As that occurs, I begin to gain some significant sense of eternity. I gain a great sense of focus, so much so, that my spirit does not stray on my journey into His presence, nor does my mind wonder. I know when I have gone behind the veil, when there is a restful silence in my spirit. I know when I have arrived in His presence, when even though I cannot see in the spirit realm with my natural eyes, I get a strong sense that there is this awesome presence before my face. I get the understanding that this presence is the Presence of the King. This is when I know that I have entered into the Presence of His Majesty.

The way I describe it to people, is to tell them to close their eyes, and I would put my hand in front of their face. Although their eyes are closed, they can still sense that something is before their face. This is the sense that I get, that tells me I have arrived into His Presence. Upon arrival, I prostrate my spirit before His throne and say nothing. I just lie there and wait. I say nothing, and I ask nothing of Him. I just lay still in my spirit and listen. After a long while of saying nothing or hearing nothing, I just tell Him that I don't mind waiting on you LORD. I would say to Him "LORD I have come to quiet my heart and still my spirit, because anything you have to say to me is far more important than anything that I have to say to you." "So speak LORD, your son hears you, and I am listening." I call it the prayer of silence. I often leave from His throne without ever asking the Father for anything.

Chapter 16

Our God is a Consuming Fire

*O*ne thing to always keep in mind, is that, in your journey into His presence, you have to ascend up to, before you enter into. Isaiah said, in the account of his vision, that he saw the LORD on His throne, and He was high and lifted up (Isaiah 6:1). He went on to say that he saw Him in His Holy Temple/Tabernacle. Judges 13:2-20 tells of the visitation, that the soon to be parents of Samson, had from an angel, before he was born. After he had finished speaking to them, they went and got a sacrifice, and offered it up on the altar unto the LORD, before the angel. As the flames went up towards heaven, the angel ascended in the flames from off the altar. Our journey into the Father's presence is an elevation of our spirit.

Anything that pertains to God has to do with fire. Any sacrifice offered to God, must ascend in fire. God does not accept strange fire. The Throne room of His Presence is characterized by coals of fire. When we pray in the spirit, we are speaking with tongues of fire. This is what the new believers experienced on the day of Pentecost in Acts 2:3-4.

This scripture states that *"there appeared unto them cloven tongues like as of fire, and it sat upon each of them. (v.4) And they were all filled with the Holy Ghost ..."* As we offer up the sacrifice of praise and worship, our spirit ascends in the fire, up to heaven and into the throne room.

When my wife and I had our first child, she had to spend a few days in the hospital because she had a Cesarean section. During that time, when I got home from work, I would put down my bag and just walk about the house, worshiping and praising God. I would do this before going to the hospital to see her. One evening, the worship got so intense, that I felt like something was literally trying to pull my spirit up out of my body. It felt like a strong force, so much so, that I got really scared. At the time, I did not know what was happening. As a result, I never did it again. I believe that if I had continued, I would have ended up having an out of body experience.

Now I have a much better understanding as to what took place. What was happening, was that my spirit was actually beginning to ascend in the fire of the sacrifice of my worship and praise. Whenever you read in the scripture about prophets seeing visions of God, and of His throne, worship is always mentioned as taking place around the throne. This is because praise and worship is intimately connected to the throne. So when we enter into the realm of praise and worship, it pulls our spirit up to His throne. When the worship that is taking place around the Throne, is also taking place in you, it causes the sea of worship to be gathered in one place. That is how your spirit rises into the realms of God, and is gathered around the Throne.

As I go behind the veil into the Throne room, I enter into the office of my priesthood consciousness/garments. In the censer of my spirit, I carry the sweet fragrance of His praise and worship. When I open the mouth of my spirit, I am allowing that sweet fragrance to ascend up to His Throne. When the priest went before the Throne, the smoke from the censer would ascend, and the fiery Presence of the LORD would descend, and rest in the cloud of that fragrant smoke, between the Cherubim. As the fiery cloud of smoke ascends up out of my spirit, then the fiery Presence of the LORD would descend in the smoke, thus creating the pillar of fire and the cloud of His presence in my life. Wherever Israel went during their wilderness years, that pillar of fire and cloud of His presence represented His abiding presence with them. During the whole life of our walk and relationship with Him, the fiery cloud of His presence, becomes His abiding Presence with us.

Chapter 17

The Attitude of the Early Community of New Covenant Believers Towards Prayer

*P*rayer was an integral and significant part of the life of the early priesthood of New Covenant Believers. In Acts 2:42, we are told that they continued steadfastly in the Apostles teaching and fellowship, and in breaking of bread, and in prayers. The adjective, *steadfastly*, means firm in purpose, resolution, unwavering, firmly established. In Greek, the word is *apoblepo* (pronounced ap-ob-lep'-o). This word means "to look away from; turn my attention". It carries the idea of turning one's attention from looking at, or being distracted by other things, just to focus on one thing. This word emphasized how serious the early believers were in committing themselves to prayer. They would not allow anything or anyone to distract them from going before God in prayer.

The Intimacy, Purpose and Power of Prayer

There is one other Greek word that I would also like to use, just to emphasize the attitude that the Early Community of New Covenant Believers held toward prayer. It is the word *proskartereo* (pronounced pros-kar-ter-eh'-o). It is a compound of two Greek words. The first part is *pros*, meaning "towards, interactively with" and *kartereo*, which means "show steadfast strength." It comes from its parent root *kratos,* which means dominion, strength, power; a mighty deed. Therefore, the word proskartereo means "to continue to do something with intense effort, with the possible implication of difficulty; to devote oneself to; to keep on, to persist in." These words, express to us the intense zeal, passion and fervency with which the early brethren practiced and lived out prayer. They understood that it is through prayer that the dominion or kingdom of God will come, and His will be done on earth, as it is in Heaven. They understood that it is through prayer that the power of the Kingdom can be exerted, and its might demonstrated.

The coming of the Holy Spirit, and the ushering in of man's redemption, came to fulfillment through prayer. Acts 2:1-2 says that *"they were all with one accord in one place. And suddenly there came a sound from heaven as of a rushing mighty wind, and it filled all the house where they were sitting."* The text does not explicitly state that they were praying, but the implication is there. What is that implication? Among the one hundred and twenty disciples who were waiting in the upper room, were the eleven Apostles of the LORD, who had asked Jesus to teach them how to pray. The Apostles no doubt led the prayer meeting, and quite possibly taught them how to pray, as Jesus had taught them.

Every four years, during the opening ceremony of the Olympics Games, the Olympic cauldron is lit with the flame from the Olympic torch, to signify the commencement of the games. To guarantee the purity of the fire, the flame of the torch is lit with the rays of the sun (Olympic.org). Before reaching its final destination in the Olympic stadium, the Olympic flame is transported to the stadium by relay.

One of the ways that the Olympic cauldron has been lit over the years, is by an archer aiming his flaming arrow at it. Once the launched arrow hits the target, it ignites, and the Olympic flames can be seen throughout the stadium. The coming of the Holy Spirit on the day of Pentecost, was the official commencement of man's redemptive race. Proverbs 20:27 states that the spirit of man is the lamp or candle of the LORD. In Hebrews 12:29, we are told that God is a consuming fire. In John 4:24, the scripture says that God is a Spirit. In 1 Corinthians 8:6, we are told that there is one God. So the one God, who is a Spirit, and a consuming fire, sent His Holy Spirit, to light the torch or lamp of man's spirit, with the fire of His Spirit. I know this to be true, because the passage states that on the day of Pentecost, there appeared unto them cloven tongues like as of fire, and it sat upon each of them. The torch was now lit, with the pure, authentic fire of God, and the redemptive relay started with 120 disciples in the upper room. That very same day, 3000 more lamps were lit, as Peter spoke with boldness and power, by the Holy Spirit. As the relay continued, more lamps were lit, as souls were added daily to the church.

All of this "moving" of the Spirit of God was financed by a praying community of believers. All of the miracles, signs and wonders were underpinned by the interceding Body of New Covenant Priesthood. So let us do what Hebrew 12:1 admonishes us to do. *"Let us lay aside every weight, and the sin which doth so easily beset us, and let us run with patience the race that is set before us."*

We read in Acts 4:29-31 that they prayed unto the LORD for boldness to speak His word, and for Him to stretch forth His hand and heal, and that signs and wonders may be done through the name of His Holy son Jesus. Verse 31 shows that results occurred immediately. The scripture states that *"when they had prayed, the place was shaken where they were assembled together; and they were all filled with the Holy*

Ghost, and they spake the word of God with boldness." The question that we need to ask ourselves today is "why does this not happen when we pray?"

We are told in Acts 12:1-17, that Peter was arrested and thrown into prison by Herod. Herod had planned to kill him after the Passover. But when the people of God began to pray for him, the scripture says that they prayed without ceasing. This caused God to move supernaturally on their behalf for Peter, and sent an angel to deliver him. The thing is, God can move so quickly and unexpectedly in response to our prayers, that when the answer shows up, we are hesitant to believe it. This is exactly what happened to the believers in this case. When Peter showed up at the door, the young woman who went to the door to ask who was knocking, got so excited when she recognized Peter's voice, that she ran to tell the others without remembering to open the door. The others, however, did not believe her. They told her it could not be, it must be an angel. Better yet, they told her that she was beside herself. In other words, girl you are hallucinating. You must be crazy. You are losing it. It was not until Peter continued knocking, that they realized that someone was really at the gate, but they only truly believed when they opened the gate, and saw him for themselves. One take-away from this miraculous account is that, we have to show stamina in our prayer life. Pray without ceasing to get results.

The Intimacy, Purpose and Power of Prayer

We read in Acts 13:1-3, that while the Community of New Covenant Believers were praying and fasting, the LORD spoke in their midst to separate unto Him Barnabas and Saul for the work that He had called them to do. This demonstrates that God reveals His will and gives us direction through prayer. The word of God, when preached in a sustained atmosphere of prayer, brings miracles, signs, and wonders.

Genesis 1:1-3 states that *"In the beginning God created the heaven and the earth. (v. 2) And the earth was without form, and void; and darkness was upon the face of the deep. And the Spirit of God moved upon the face of the waters. (v. 3) And God said, Let there be light: and there was light."* Physicists and scientists tell us that everything in the earth exists within an electromagnetic energy field. They said that this magnetic energy field is what gives sustenance, and the maintenance of life to everything on earth. This is because everything on earth lives in that light. So when God said let there be light, He was creating the electromagnetic field that would sustain the life of everything that He created. Prayer creates that spiritual electromagnetic atmosphere of power in the spirit, in which God operates and work. As long as that atmospheric energy field of prayer is charged and sustained, the Kingdom of God will have an open portal for manifestation and demonstration.

The early believers understood that their approach or attitude toward prayer must be one of calculated, sustained effort. They exhibited a passionate and fiery disposition in seeking the LORD in prayer. Effectual and fervent prayers opened up the Heavens, and kept it opened. They understood that nothing can happen in the earth under a closed Heaven. They understood that as long as the Heavens were kept open, Satan's kingdom would come under unrelenting waves of invasion, and unending barrage of attacks. The problem, however, was that Satan knew that too.

A fetus lives in the womb and is connected to its source, which is the mother, by way of the umbilical cord. This is how food from the mother gets to the fetus, and this is how waste from the fetus leaves his body. The early believers understood that the womb of prayer was the environment in which they needed to live and be sustained. It was their umbilical cord of faith that connected them to their Heavenly source. They realized that the maintenance of this atmosphere was how they could penetrate the Heavens, and how the Heavens could penetrate the earth. They realized that these two major factors had to be present in order for God to work, or exert His power. These two atmospheres of prayer and faith were a sustained, present and resident reality in the life of the Community of New Covenant Believers. It allowed for the birthing of God's purpose.

The Intimacy, Purpose and Power of Prayer

Hebrews 11:6 underscores that along with prayer, the atmosphere of faith must be present in order for our prayers to be effective. It plainly states that without faith, it is impossible to please God. The scripture further qualifies this statement by saying that *"for he that cometh to God must believe that he is, and that he is a rewarder of them that diligently seek him."* In approaching the Father, we must possess an attitude of faith.

Mark 6:5-6 gives us an example of the disservice that we cause ourselves, when we lack faith in God. The atmosphere of faith was not present in Capernaum, therefore, the works that Jesus did there were severely limited to only a few. He was only able to lay hands on a few sick people and heal them. The word says that Jesus marveled at their unbelief. Jesus was awestruck, and not in a good way. He went back to His own country to teach the people, but did not find many who would receive Him in faith.

The same thing happens with some believers today. We go to the house of God with little or no expectation of what the LORD will do in our services. When God does "show up" or manifest himself in our midst, we are not prepared to receive Him. There are times that the minister have to work hard to get the people excited and enthusiastic about worshipping the King. That shows the people's lack of personal relationship with the Father. Therefore, many believers leave the house of God empty and even frustrated, because they only had a religious experience, and not an encounter with the Father.

As the Body of Christ today, unlike our earlier counterpart, we are living in the Capernaum age. They were living under an open heaven, whereby they experienced a strong current and flow of the Holy Spirit. We are living under an ajar heaven, and only experience a trickle and a drip. We are living in the "not many mighty works" age, rather than in the "greater works than these shall you do" age. Due to the fact, that as the Body of Christ, we are not operating or functioning in such sustained atmospheres in our times, it would give the impression that the Devil is subtracting and dividing, more than the LORD is adding and multiplying.

Another difference between the early Community of New Covenant Believers and us today is that they had the Fire of God. The fire that consumed and burned up the sacrifice that was on the brazen altar, came down from the LORD according to 2 Chronicles 7:1, 1 Kings 18:38 and Leviticus 9:24. The fire that lit the altar of incense, and the golden candle sticks, came from the brazen altar of sacrifice. The fire that filled the golden censer, came from the altar of incense as stated in Leviticus 16:12. Any fire that was used to light anything in the tabernacle, had to come from the LORD as its source. Any fire that was offered before the LORD, and He was not the source, was called strange fire.

The bearer who offered up strange fire would die. This was the case with the two sons of Aaron in Leviticus 10:1-2. The fire of the LORD would descend to confirm that the offered up sacrifice by the high priest, was acceptable. We also see this in the account of Elijah and the prophets of Baal. The descending fire of God on the day of Pentecost also communicated the same thing. It was to confirm that the sacrifice of His son Jesus was acceptable. The fire is missing today, because the acceptable sacrifice is also missing. Somewhere in the passage of time, the fire from Heaven, that was used to light the torch or lamp of our spirit, went out. So today, while we encourage people to pray, many will not. Efforts are made to promote soul winning and evangelism, but this is met with a lackluster response. All sorts of gimmicks and strategies have been employed in order to get people excited about doing things for the LORD. However, in most cases, there is little or no result. This is nothing but strange fire that we are bringing before the LORD.

We are not getting the same results as did our brethren in the Book of Acts. The difference between us and them is the fire, the prayer, and the one accord, or having all things common. The result of such differences is that the early New

The Attitude of the Early Community of
New Covenant Believers Towards Prayer

Testament Believers demonstrated the power, then directed the people to the power source. We today, preach about the power without demonstration, thus obscuring the visual of the power source. We have to move from preaching the power, to preaching the power into full demonstration.

In summing up this portion, I will use four attributes to characterize the early New Covenant Believers.

(i)   They had a strong and sustained prayer life.
(ii) They were bold and fierce in their pursuit of prayer.
(iii) They had a spirit of community.
(iv) They lived a life of demonstrated power and kingdom authority.

They were able to do this because not only were they convinced in their own hearts about who God is, but they worked in unity to relay the fire of God to the next potential group of believers.

Now allow me to make it unequivocally clear. This is not an indictment or a condemnation of the Body of Christ. It is merely an observation of the posture of present day believers, from an historical perspective. The question is, "What happened?" What has made the Body of Christ so unrecognizable today in comparison to the early believers? What interrupted that strong current and fluent flow of the operation of the Spirit? What caused the prayer fountain to dry up? What has stolen our boldness? What broke up the sense of community? What has left the Body of Christ in the state and condition in which we now find ourselves today? The answer to these questions is twofold. I will share my perspective in the next section.

Chapter 18

How Did We Get Here From There and How Do We Get Back There From Here

The Backsliding

*T*here are two steps that have led us on this downward path. They are, the spirit of religion, and the spirit of worldly culture. We see in the scriptures, time and time again, how Israel turned away from God, because of the culture and religion of the surrounding nations. This was because the religious practices of the Hittites, Ammonites, Amorites and the other Caananite nations were able to enter Israel's spiritual life. These nations worshipped idols such as Molech, Eshtar and Baal. Israel was greatly influenced by the fashion, philosophy, ideology and worldview of these idolaters. As a result, they began to lose their distinctiveness and identity that kept them separate from these nations.

The consequence of Israel turning away from God was that they were displaced from their land, and carried off into captivity by other nations. Israel, which was made up of ten tribes of the northern Kingdom, was carried off into captivity by the Assyrians. The southern Kingdom of Judah was carried off in three different deportations, to Babylon. By the time Jesus came on the scene, only the southern Kingdom of Judah had returned to the Promised Land. That is why Jesus told His disciples in the gospels that He was sent to the lost sheep of the House of Israel.

We read in Judges 2:7-10, that Israel served God all the days of Joshua, and all the days of the elders who outlived Joshua, and had seen all the great works of the LORD that He did for Israel. However, after these had died out, the scripture goes on to say that another generation came after them that did not know God. This is why Gideon asked the angel of the LORD who spoke with him in Judges 6:13, *"Oh my LORD, if the LORD be with us, why then is all this befallen us?"* Gideon was basically saying that, if God is with us, why do we live in this condition? Where are all the miracles that our fathers told us of….? We see this same paradigm or model to be the reality of the spiritual Israel of God of our times. That is the thought

How Did We Get Here From There and How Do We Get Back There From Here

provoking question that we as the Body Christ should be asking ourselves today. Where are the miracles, signs, and wonders that we read about in the Book of Acts? Where is the resurrection power that we read about, that was demonstrated by Peter and Paul, to name just a few? Where is the manifestation of the Glory, and demonstration of the Kingdom that we read about? Where are the greater works that we will do? Jesus will teach us, but somebody has to ask Him. He will show us the way, but someone has to cry out in hunger and longing first, to release His arm of salvation. Indeed, Israel got her deliverance, but someone had to cry out first.

A part of the backsliding of the Body of Christ took place from within. In 2 Timothy 3:1-7, Paul warned that the time would come when people would not endure sound doctrine or teaching, but after their own lusts will heap to themselves teachers, having itching ears. They will turn away their ears from the truth, and will turn to fables. The word for fable in the Greek is *muthos/mythos* (pronounced moo-thos), which is defined as a myth; a false account, yet posing to be the truth; a fabrication (fable) which subverts (replaces) what is actually true. This state eventually leads to what Paul describes as having a form of godliness, but denying the power thereof. The word deny in Greek is *aparneomai* (pronounced ap-ar-neh-om-ahee). It is the compound of the prefix *apó*, which means "from". It intensifies the word to which it is attached.

Arneomai means "deny; refuse to affirm or to confess (identify with); disown (repudiate)." So *aparnéomai* suggests "strongly reject". So Paul was in essence saying that they would strongly reject identifying with Christ or the cross. They would no longer recognize God as the source of power, and they would live in a way that would contradict the testimony, and life of Christ that they once lived. This really means that the time would come when they would no longer manifest or demonstrate the power of God.

Genesis 2 said that God formed man out of the dust of the ground. Without the breath of God, all man had was just a form, without the power of life. When God breathed His breath of life into the form of man, that form then had the power of life, and became a living, thinking, speaking, being. For the Body of Christ to have a form of godliness, but no power, is to have religion.

In Acts 2, on the day of Pentecost, that rushing mighty wind that they experienced in the upper room, was actually God breathing His breath of life into the Body, or form of His son Jesus. As a result, the Body, or form of Christ was given the power of life, and became a living, speaking, demonstrative expression of the Christ being in the earth. That is why Jesus told His Body, or form, to remain in the dust of the upper room, until they received power that the world could not deny. This undeniable power, would serve as the foundation, from which Paul warned, that the Body of Christ would be removed. Paul warned us of the religious cloak, clothing, or carnal nature that the Community of New Covenant Believers would take on as a result of this departure.

In denying the power, the Body of Christ would lose or forfeit kingdom impact, influence, credibility, and relevance. In anointing Saul to be king over Israel, in 1 Samuel 10:6, Samuel prophesied to him that the Spirit of the LORD shall come upon him, and he shall be turned into another man. In verse 9, it states that when he turned his back to go from Samuel, God gave him another heart. In verse 7 Samuel told him that God was with him. So we see here that Saul went from having a national religion, to a personal relationship with the LORD. That is, Saul went from knowing God on a corporate level, to knowing him personally. However, as a result of his disobedience later on, Saul was rejected, and lost his relationship with the LORD. He remained king, or kept his form, but had no power of relationship.

After God rejected Saul, He sent Samuel to anoint another man by the name of David (1 Samuel 16:13). David was the eighth son of Jesse. The number eight represents a new thing or new beginning. The verse says that after Samuel anointed him, the Spirit of the LORD came upon David from that day forward. The passage goes on to say that the Spirit of the LORD departed from Saul, and an evil spirit from the LORD troubled him. As a result, Saul turned to inquire of witches, because Samuel was dead and he was no longer hearing from the LORD. In chapter 15:25, after God had rejected Saul, (before Samuel's death), he wanted Samuel to turn again with him, so he could worship the LORD. This request was out of a religious spirit. Religion will always seek to get validation and legitimacy from something that is legitimate. Religion will always try to use past legitimacy, for present validation. He knew that he would lose all legitimate claim, if the people were to find out that the LORD had rejected him.

Saul represented a religious system. He represented what God was doing, and where God was coming from. David represented the relationship of what God was currently doing, and where He was going next. Saul's relationship became a religion when he lost approval or endorsement of being selected and anointed by God. He lost what I call the "God factor". David's relationship became confirmed, when he gained the "God factor."

When Saul put his battle clothing on David, it was equivalent to religion trying to clothe or cover over the true relationship with Christ. David attempted to go, but turned back and took them off. He told Saul that he could not go to

fight in that armor, because he had not proven them. In
essence, David told Saul that he did not need religion, because
he had relationship. He was saying that he would fight in the
armor of his relationship, because he had proven that armor.

We read the narrative in 1 King 18:19-20, concerning the
showdown between the prophets of the religion of Baal and
Elijah, the relationship prophet of Yahweh. Elijah threw down
the gauntlet, and put the challenge out there. He named the
place and time for the showdown between him and the
prophets of Baal. They met on the Mount of Carmel. He
allowed them to go first. They chanted and cried out to Baal
from the morning to the evening. It came to the point where
they got so desperate for a response from their idol that they
jumped upon the altar and began to cut themselves. As the
blood began to gush forth, they began to cry louder. To add
insult to injury, Elijah began to mock them. He demonstrated
a level of confidence and boldness. When he finally had
enough, he told them to stop the shenanigans, and step aside.
He was now going to establish who the true God was, "the one
that answers by fire." He had them set up the sacrifice upon
the altar, and saturate it, along with the ground around it,
with twelve barrels of water. Then he called upon God. Not
only did God answer by fire, but the water that was upon, and
around the altar, was also consumed. Elijah was able to be that
bold and confident, because he had relationship with God, and

not religion. Relationship challenged religion, and defeated it unequivocally.

We read in 1 Chronicles 16:1-40, that although David had removed the Ark of God to Jerusalem, and the Presence of God had departed, the priests still remained and offered up sacrifice both day and night. That was where God used to be, but when His presence was no longer there, all they had was a religious system, void of Presence and Glory. So here we have a system that had historical legitimacy, but no present validation.

In the account of David and Goliath, Saul was present with his armor on, but he was still afraid to go out and fight Goliath. Religion will cause you to look the part, but have no heart for God, people, or the Glory of God. The Ark of God's Presence was taken on Saul's watch. In the forty years that Saul was king over Israel, there is no mention or evidence in the scripture that he ever tried, or made any attempt to go after, or restore the Glory. He spent all of his waking time pursuing and chasing after David. What have been lost on your watch, that you have not gone after, because you are preoccupied with chasing after other things, instead of chasing after God? Religion will cause you to chase after man, and not after God. Religion will give you a form of godliness, but rob you of the power. This was the sickness that eventually plagued The New

How Did We Get Here From There and How Do We Get Back There From Here

Covenant believers of early times. When you embrace religion, it will cripple you, because it does not possess the strength to carry you.

We read in 2 Samuel 4:4, of the incident concerning Saul and Jonathan. When the nurse for Jonathan's son received news that Saul and Jonathan were dead, she picked up

Mephibosheth, the son of Jonathan, and began to run with him. As she fled in haste, she dropped him. This accident left him crippled. However, as a result of his father's relationship with King David, a permanent place was prepared for him at the king's table. If the religious will humble themselves at the table of relationship, then they can be fed and sustained.

In Matthew 4:8-9, we are told that Satan took Jesus up into an exceeding high mountain, and showed him all the kingdoms of the world, and the glory of them. He offered to give them all to Jesus, if He would fall down and worship him. When Satan saw that he could not prevail, he left Jesus for a season. Whatever proposition that he made to the Head, he will also make to the Body. Satan returned in a season of severe persecution, and made the same offer again to the Body of Christ. The Body of Christ accepted the offer, and in doing so traded the Kingdom of God's power and impact, for worldly political power and influence. This resulted in a severe break, or separation between the Head and His Body.

The Babylonian Deception

The Babylonian Mystery Religion, was the religious system founded by the Babylonians. It included an elaborate and very complex priesthood. The Medes and Persian Empire invaded, and eventually conquered Babylon the Great. Although the priesthood was maintained for a while, they were forced to flee Babylon as the result of a rebellion. Upon leaving Babylon, they came to settle in the Kingdom of Pergamum. It became the established religion of the kingdom. The king was not just the Head of State. He was also the head or high priest of the Babylonian Mystery Religion. He was not just the king, but he also bore the title of Pontifex Maximus.

In 133 B.C., the last king of Pergamum, Attalus the Third, surrendered this title to the Roman emperor. In 63 A.D, Julius Caesar was appointed Emperor. By this time, he was already functioning as Pontifex Maximus. He was now serving as both priest and king (hope-of-israel.org). Every emperor from Julius Caesar onward, served in this dual capacity. At this time, Pergamum ceased to be an independent political entity, and became a province of the Roman Empire. The term *pontifex* was used to describe the five Roman (pagan) priests, who constituted the headship of the religious system. The head of this council was called Pontifex Maximus, which means high priest of the pagans/heathens (Conte, R.). The Christian

How Did We Get Here From There and How Do We Get Back There From Here

Emperor of Rome, by the name of Gratian, in the 4th century, turned down the title of Pontifex Maximus. In May of 325 A.D., Constantine the First, emperor and Pontifex Maximus of the Roman Empire, called an ecumenical council to discuss and settle the doctrinal disagreements that were dividing Christianity within the Roman Empire. This was the opened door that allowed doctrinal heresy to enter the Body of Christ.

In 378 A.D., the Bishop of Rome, named Damascus, accepted the title of Pontifex Maximus for himself, and was elected to this position (hope-of-israel.org). This led the Body of Christ into further decay and corruption.

In the Edict of Milan, in 313 A.D., Emperor Constantine made Christianity an acceptable religion in the Empire. Emperor Theodosius the First, in 380 A.D., by the Edict of Thessalonica, made the Roman version of Christianity, formulated at the council of Nicene, the state religion of the empire. He permanently stopped "state sponsorship of any form of paganism." In 393 A.D., he enacted more laws opposing any form of pagan religion, at which time he also ended the Roman Olympic tradition. Christianity had now achieved political power and social influence, and was now on top of the proverbial food chain. With this new status, came a transfer of the rights and privileges that the other former state religions once enjoyed. Not to be denied, many pagans from the other religions in the empire feigned conversion to Christianity, in order to continue enjoying those rights and privileges. When they came into this new state religion, with unconverted hearts, they brought their pagan beliefs, and worldview with them. With process of time, Christianity became more structured, and more organized, by becoming a state religion. That positioned Christianity under the headship of the state/emperor. As a result, the state had a lot of influence, or say, in how this new State religion would function. This brought about a major shift in Christ Centered Christianity, and the Community of New Covenant Believers went from being a living organism, to a religious organization. It also shifted them from under the Headship of Christ, to the headship of man. Roman Catholic Christianity was now fully born and fully grown.

The Body of Christ was now fully clothed in the garments, or clothing of religion. The headship of man that now sits atop of a decapitated Body of Christ, is called Pope. This comes from *papa* in the Greek, and is translated as *father* in English. This is a direct violation of Jesus' command in Matthew 23:9, that we should call no man on earth our father, because we only have one Father, which is in heaven. This person is also called "the vicar of Christ". This word is derived from Latin *vicarious,* which is interpreted as "instead of" (gotquestions.org). So as the Vicar of Christ, this person is to be accepted instead of Christ, as one equal with Christ. This is why this religion practices confession, because it is the belief that the priest can absolve a follower from their sins. That is why they believe that in matters of the church and doctrine, the Pope is infallible. This corrupt version of Christianity erroneously bases or validates its legitimacy on the legitimate and heavenly sanctioned Apostleship of Peter. Their claim is that Peter was the first Pope. Their anchor text for this false assumption is Matthew 16:18-19, where Christ gave Peter the keys of the Kingdom of Heaven. Anything that has to do with Babylon, carries a curse.

We read in Joshua 7:21, where an Israelite by the name of Achan stole a Babylonian garment, with some gold and silver. He hid them in his tent in the heart of the earth. It brought Israel to a standstill, and a major defeat before their enemy. He and his whole house were stoned to death. Being clothed in the garment of religion, is having on the Babylonian garment, which has led to the death of bible truths, and the death of the fluent flow of the Holy Spirit. It is also responsible for the putting out of the Fire of God, in the Body of Christ in our times. It has also brought the Kingdom of God to a crawl, or seeming standstill, in terms of sustained, and fluent Kingdom manifestation and demonstration in power.

The other curse that the Community of New Covenant

The Intimacy, Purpose and Power of Prayer

Believers experienced, was that of leprosy. We read in 2 Kings 5:27, how Gehazi went after Naaman the Syrian, to collect the gifts that Elisha had refused at his hands, after Naaman was healed from leprosy. Upon Gehazi's return to the house, Elisha questioned him as to where he was coming from. He lied and said he did not go anywhere. Elisha, knowing that Gehazi was lying, pronounced the curse of leprosy over him and his seed. He went out from the presence of Elisha with full blown leprosy. In this context, Elisha is Christ the head, Gehazi is the Body of Christ, Naaman is the world, and the silver, gold and garments are the things of the world. When the Body of Christ chose to leave Christ, and go after the world, and the things of the world, they became plagued with the same sickness of the world.

This sickness that plagues the world and religion, is the disease of leprosy. Leprosy is a disease that damages, or destroys the peripheral nerves (nerves outside the brain and spinal cord), skin, testes, eyes, and mucus membranes of the nose and throat. People with leprosy can be severely disfigured, and disabled. If not timely, or properly treated it can lead to death. A person who is plagued with this disease in their body, stands to lose all sense of feeling. So if they were to unknowingly say for example, put their hand in fire, they would not feel any pain. The fact that they do not feel the pain, does not negate the damage, harm, or loss that their body, or body member would suffer.

How Did We Get Here From There and How Do We Get Back There From Here

The Body of Christ in our times is suffering from spiritual leprosy. Our spiritual nerves, which is our spiritual sense of discernment, has become dull and numb. This sickness does not allow us to discern spiritual things. Spiritual leprosy is the sin of carnality. In 1 Corinthians 2:14, Paul says that the natural or carnal man receives not the things of the Spirit of God, for they are foolishness unto him. Neither can he know them, because they are spiritually discerned. That is why the world, or religion cannot discern or know spiritual things, because they are carnal to it, and those things are foolishness to them. That is why the world, or religion cannot walk before God, because spiritual leprosy has made them disabled, and has marred or disfigured the image of Christ to them. Having such sickness, as the Body of Christ, has dulled and numbed our discernment and sensitivity to the Fire of God's presence, leading, guidance, instructions, or direction. It makes us numb to what is right, just, good, or what is righteous from God's perspective.

The spirit of religion and worldliness, is the unified weight that is resting on the Body of Christ in our times. That is why the author of Hebrews 12:1 implores us to lay aside every weight, and the sin that so easily beset us. The verb *"weight"* means to hold (something) down by placing a heavy object on top of it. The word *beset* means to surround; harass; assail on all sides; to hem in. So we should discard or put off the weight of worldliness and religion that surrounds us, and aggressively pressure us to conform, thereby making it difficult, or even impossible for us to advance the will and purpose of God in the earth. When the Body of Christ was bound with the new ropes of religion and worldliness, we became weak and powerless, thus becoming a religion just like any other worldly religion.

Samson played and toyed with Delilah until he finally fell asleep in her lap. She called for the symbol of his strength to be taken, which was his hair. The two things that Samson lost that day were his eyes and his hair. These speak of his anointing and his vision. As the Body of Christ, we have fallen asleep, or lost spiritual consciousness in the lap of Delilah. The lap is formed by both legs of an individual, in a sitting posture. From this posture, it begins at the knee and ends at the top of the thigh. The lap of Delilah speaks of the two legs of worldliness and religion. Delilah comes from the Hebrew root *del* which means "who weakens or eradicates; weak or poor. The word *eradicate* means to destroy completely; put an end to. That is what Satan, through worldliness and religion, has been doing to the Body of Christ.

The story, however, is not yet finished. There is a remnant that is seeking the Holy One for the unadulterated Fire of God, to rekindle the flame of the spirit of man. God will arise and cause His enemies to scatter. In time, God will arise and lead captivity captive. In time, the Glory of the LORD shall rise up on His Body, and like the bones in the valley of dry bones, we shall live again.

In the fullness of time we will be healed of our leprosy. Our hair will grow back, and we will receive our sight, and our spiritual consciousness. In time we will continue to do all that Jesus began both to do and teach, and the greater works than these will we do. The weight of God, is the Glory of God. The word *glory* in Hebrews means weighty or heavy. We need God to show up in His Body/Temple once again, and throw His weight around, let His Mighty Presence be known, and let His power lose under the whole Heavens, to His praise and glory.

Now that we understand a little about how we got here from there, we also need to understand how to get back there from here.

The Return
(Natural Israel)

In 2 Chronicles 7:14, in speaking to Israel, the LORD said to them, *"If my people, which are called by my name, shall*

The Intimacy, Purpose and Power of Prayer

humble themselves, and pray, and seek my face, and turn from their wicked ways; then will I hear from heaven, and will forgive their sin, and will heal their land."

Let us examine this verse of scripture. In ancient Israel, when they wanted to seek God, they would humble themselves by afflicting their souls through fasting. They would wear sackcloth, which consisted of a coarse material that was usually made of goat's hair. There was no inner lining, so the material would irritate or agitate their skin, whether they wore it, or spread it under them in ashes. There is a wrong and a right way to fast. The reason why God did not hear Israel in Isaiah 58:3, was because they were praying religious, self-righteous, self-centered and hypocritical prayers. The fasting that God finds acceptable, however, is stated in Isaiah 58:6-7.

If you noticed, the first thing that God said that they must do after humbling themselves, was to pray. Praying was the very first thing that was done in the upper room that brought down the fiery presence of God. As it was in the beginning, so shall it be in the end. In 2 Chronicles 7:14, God made them to understand that the only kind of prayer that He will hear, is prayer that is God centric, Kingdom oriented, and faith based.

To *seek* means to search out, pursue, go after with focus, steadfastness and directed intentionality. God said that it is

How Did We Get Here From There and How Do We Get Back There From Here

His face that they must seek. *Face,* in scripture, speaks of personal intimacy and relationship. God was telling Israel that they should pursue, or go after a personal relationship with Him, rather than going after Him for things, or for what He could do for them. He was telling them to seek His ways, and not His hand. The hand speaks of strength or power. It also speaks of what He can do.

The LORD then told them that they should turn from their wicked ways. This was a call to repentance. The Hebrew word for repent is *teshuva,* which means to return. By implication, it means to turn from, and back to. When it is God calling for *teshuva,* He is calling His people back from sin to the paths of righteousness. Teshuva not only means to repent, but it also means answer. In calling His people to repent, God was letting them know that He was giving them the answer or solution to their sin sick state and condition. He was letting them know that for them to repent, or to turn back to Him, was the answer.

Wicked ways in this context speaks of depravity of character, and a loss of moral compass and direction. Their wicked ways spoke of the actions, attitude, behavior or conduct that was evidence of their departure from God. When the LORD spoke of *"my people, which are called by my name",* He was referring to people who had the identity of His nature or character. The word *"name"* in Hebrew is *shem*. It is not simply an identifier for a person, but it speaks of the essence of a person's being, or the core of their character, which goes to the truth of who they really are.

So when God said they are called by His name, He was in essence saying that they are identified with the character of who He is, by way of covenant. Covenant was made by two people cutting a sacrifice in two, and then both parties would walk between the sacrifice. This act was to bear witness between the two parties, that they are now bound by covenant to the agreement that they just entered into. We see evidence of this example in Genesis 15:10, where God told Abraham the kind of sacrifice that he was to prepare before Him. Then the bible said that he took all the sacrifices, and divided them in the midst, or he cut them in two. In verse 12, God caused a deep sleep to come upon Abraham, and then God began to prophesy to him concerning his future, and concerning the destiny of his seed. In verse 17, we are told that when the sun went down, and it was dark, behold a smoking furnace, and a burning lamp that passed between those pieces.

So what God was saying to Israel in 2 Chronicles 7:14, was that they were joined together as one, but they were not reflecting His ways, nor were they doing His character justice by their wicked ways. He was letting them know that His

character was the dominant gene in their relationship, and
that was what they were to reflect, rather than reflecting the
recessive gene of their unrighteousness.

God told Israel that if they turned from their wicked ways
and sought His face, then He would hear from heaven. The
word *hear* in Hebrew is *shema* (pronounced sheh'-mah). It
means to actively listen and pay close attention, with the
intent to understand and to comply with what is heard. It
means to take action that corresponds with what you hear. The
LORD said that heaven is His throne and the earth is His foot
stool. The throne is the seat of a king's legitimacy. It is the
place from which he exercises absolute power and authority.
Therefore, when the LORD said that He would hear from
heaven, He was letting Israel know that not only would He pay
close attention to what they asked of Him, but He was also in
the place of absolute power and authority to help them. He
was letting them know that repentance would bring them into
the posture for them to receive His help.

The LORD also told them that He would forgive their sin.
The word *forgive* in Hebrew means to cover over. It is what we
call atonement in English. It conveys that the one who was the
victim of the offense, chooses not to see the offense of the
offender. To not cover over the offense, is to hold the offender
guilty, and then in turn require justice or retribution. The

whole concept of forgiveness carries the idea of restoration or resumption of relationship, once atonement has been made. God was letting Israel know that He would cover over their sin, and not exact retribution against them. He would release them from their offense against Him, so that there could be a restoration of their covenant relationship.

The word *sin* in Hebrew means to miss the mark. It was an archery term that was used to indicate when an archer failed to hit his target. It would be said of him, that he sinned. God's mark for Israel was for them to be the reflection of His character to the heathen nations who were all around them. It was for them to be the light to people who were sitting in the darkness of sin and unrighteousness. Their wickedness caused them to miss the mark, and to fail.

In continuing to look at 2 Chronicles 7:14, when the LORD said that He would heal their land, what would the land need to be healed from? In verse 13 of the same chapter, the LORD said what the land would be cursed with. He mentioned drought, locusts and pestilence. So by implication, what the land was cursed with, is what it would be healed from. For the land to be in drought, means that there was no rain. For them not to have any rain, meant that heaven was closed. That was the LORD's way of protesting their wickedness.

How Did We Get Here From There and How Do We Get Back There From Here

The Hebrew word for "to heal" is *rapha* (pronounced raw-faw). This word carries the idea of restoring back to health; to make whole to the point where nothing is broken or nothing is missing. Inherent in this word, is the idea of protection. So restoring the health of the land would call for God to reopen the heavens, and cause it to rain again. This would mean that their whole agricultural system would be brought back into balance, upon which their livelihood and economy depended. Because the sickness of the land was the curse of drought, in healing the land, He was by implication saying that He would protect them from the curse, if they protected His glory from wickedness. He finally ended His plea with Israel by assuring them, that if they heard His call to them to return, then He would in turn open His eyes to their plight, and His ears to their call. He was reassuring them, that if they returned to Him, then He would also return to them, and would recognize them as His people. He would also reaffirm Himself as their God once again.

(Spiritual Israel)

We read in the book of Revelation, (Revelation 2:4-15), where Jesus addressed the seven different Community of New Covenant Believers, who were located in Asia Minor. There were many other churches in the Roman Empire at the time, such as the Corinthians, Galatians, Philippians, etc. Nevertheless, it was only these seven churches that Jesus addressed. Why? These churches were what I call anchor churches, because they were in major cities in the empire. This meant that what happened in those seven churches would influence the other churches throughout the empire.

The first of the seven churches that He wrote to was the church in Ephesus. Ephesus was the fourth largest city in the eastern hemisphere of the Roman Empire in the 2nd century B.C. It was famous for being the sight for the temple and shrine of Artemis/Diana, and it was also renowned for its medical school. After praising them for their strength, the LORD's indictment against them was that they left their first love. He admonished them to repent, and do the first works again, or face severe judgment. The word repent in the Greek is a compound word *metanoeó* (pronounced met-an-o-eh-o), which is made up of *meta* and *noiéō*. *Meta* means "changed after being with", and *noiéō* means "think". The combination of these words gives the meaning to "think differently after"; "after a change of mind". So repent literally means to "think differently afterwards". Thinking differently afterwards is the effect, evidence, or result of changing one's mind, which in turn will cause you to go in a different or new direction. So when Jesus told them to repent, He was actually telling them to change their course of action or direction, through a changed heart and mind. The first works speaks of doing the things that brought them into relationship in the beginning. This would have brought them back to their initial state of intimacy with Him.

The LORD also took issue with the church in Pergamos. They were indicted with "a few things", according to the LORD.

(i) They gave room to the doctrine of the Nicolaitans, which the LORD said He hated. The word *Nicolaitans* is the compound of three Greek words.

These words are:

(a) Niko, which means a conquest; subdue; victory; triumph; those who dominate over the defeated.

(b) *Lai, Laos* which means people

(c) *tes* or *ton* which means *the.*

So the word Nicolaitans means the conqueror of the people.

The LORD said to them, that they seem to have given place to something that He hated. This thing, He said, are the deeds of the Nicolaitans. The word *hate* in the Greek is *miseo (pronounced mis-eh'-o),* which means to abhor; or to find utterly repulsive; hate. It describes the deep rooted animosity of a person. It means to loathe or reject completely. It carries the idea of extreme disgust and hostility towards. Jesus was expressing His hatred for the deeds of the Nicolaitans on the same level as His hatred for sin. Their deeds were all inclusive of their behavior, actions, beliefs, and whatever else was associated with them.

Irenaeus and Hippolytus, were two leaders in the early church, who recorded that the Nicolaitans were a heretical sect. They were spiritual successors of Nicolas of Antioch. Nicolas was one of the seven Deacons, who were chosen by the people, and brought before the Apostles, in Acts 6:5. Nicolas' background was steeped in pagan roots. He was a proselyte who converted from Paganism to Judaism, and then from Judaism to Christianity. They said that he "taught a doctrine of compromise" and he believed that absolute separation between Christianity and paganism was not necessary. So Nicolas created a mixture of Christian with pagan teaching, which he did in the name of Christian liberty. In doing so, he conquered, and subdued the faith of many in the church (renner.org). This is why we can see God's strong reaction to the behavior of the church in adopting these beliefs.

It was one of extreme disgust and loathing. God absolutely hated it.

    (ii)   Jesus rebuked the church in Pergamos not just for the Nicolaitans heresy, but also for the heresy of Balaam.

How Did We Get Here From There and How Do We Get Back There From Here

The reference to Baalam goes back to the Old Testament in Numbers 22:1-41. It is the account of when Israel was journeying through the wilderness after leaving Egypt. The narrative tells us that when Balak, the king of Moab, saw all what Israel did to the Amorites, and saw that they were great in numbers, he became afraid. In order to defeat Israel, he called a soothsayer by the name of Baalam to curse them. After inquiring of the LORD, Baalam was told not to go. However, the king increased his offer of wealth, with a promise of promotion also. The offer was so tempting, that Baalam went back to enquire of the LORD again. God gave him the go ahead this time around, even though it was not His will. However, He instructed Baalam, that he was do as He (God) told him. Baalam still had his own agenda. So when the king brought him to the plains of Moab and showed him the children of Israel, he opened his mouth to curse them. However, every time that Balaam tried to curse them, a blessing came out. He was, determined to get his reward regardless. So he told Balak how to get them to sin against God, and be cursed by Him. The plan was to get the children of Israel commit fornication with the Moabites, and to eat meat offered to idols. The plan succeeded, because Israel did just that, and sinned against God.

Since Balaam prostituted his gift to gain prestige and influence, and Jesus referenced him in his address to the church in Pergamos, it is fair to say that covetousness was part of the heresy. So the doctrine of Balaam, or what Balaam taught by his actions, speaks of people who use their gift or ministry for material gain, or power and position. If you noticed, in the account of Balaam, he still tried to maintain a relationship with God, while trying to get the wealth of the Moabite king. It is dangerous to try to keep a relationship with God, while colluding with the enemy, to gain what you have your eyes on in his camp. This will eventually lead to your destruction and to the hurt of those who are affected by your ministry. So the spirit of Baalam in the Pergamos church was the spirit of covetousness and compromise.

(iii)   In Revelation 2:13, Jesus told the church there, that they dwell where Satan's throne is.

There are few reasons that would lead Him to make that statement. First of all, Pergamos was the home of the priests of the Babylonian Mystery Religion. They were its guardians or custodians. They settled there after fleeing from Babylon. They were the rulers of the Kingdom of Pergamum through the Attalic Dynasty. It was in Pergamum where the first temple for emperor worship, was built, thus becoming the main center of emperor worship. It was the seat of the cults of Zeus, Athena, Dionysus, and Asclepius. The idol Asclepius was in the form of a serpent. He was called the savior healer (Walvoord, J.F.).

How Did We Get Here From There and How Do We Get Back There From Here

Interestingly enough, the name Pergamos is a compound of the two Greek words, *per* and *gamos*. *Per* is derived from *perí,* which means fully concerning; wholly, very, really. *Per* is used to emphasize the word it is attached to, therefore, it is given the meaning thoroughly. *Gamos* means a wedding; marriage festival; a wedding banquet; a wedding feast; marriage or matrimony. So putting the two together gives the meaning of Pergamos to be *thoroughly wedded.* So Jesus' grave concern was that the Pergamum church was mixing with the world to such an extent that it became a marriage.

The conclusion to this discussion is that the church at Pergamos lost their chastity. They cohabitated with the world through compromise and false teaching, thereby defiling their relationship with God. They prostituted their gift, by going in the way of Baalam, and they gave up eternal promises for temporary satisfaction and gratification. This marriage between the world, religion and the church led to "Christianity being heathenized, and to heathenism being Christianized", according to the Roman emperor's version of Christianity. This meant that pagan temples were converted over to Christian churches, pagan festivals were changed into Christian feasts, and pagan priests were deceitfully passed off as Christian priests.

The lesson for us today is that we should guard our relationship with the Father. We can deceive ourselves into thinking that we can have the "best of both worlds". This happens when our view gets distorted. We see what's in the world as very desirable, so we deceive ourselves into believing that since we can still pray and hear from God, our relationship with Him is intact. This, while our hearts lust after what is in the world. God firmly rejected this belief and called for His people to repent. If we go after God, He has to be our sole desire. He promised that if we seek first the Kingdom and His righteousness, then all that we are in need of will be added to us, because He knows what we have need of.

In Joel 2:12-13, the LORD commanded Israel to return to Him with all of their heart, and with fasting, and with weeping, and with mourning. He told them to rend their hearts and not their garment. He was letting them know that any action taken in order to get His attention, that does not include the heart, is nothing but pure religion. He was telling them not to rend their garments to expose their nakedness but instead rend their heart and open it to him. He was in essence telling them that he does not want their body if he cannot have their heart.

In Zechariah 3:1, the prophet describes a vision that he had experienced. In this vision he saw Joshua, the high priest, standing before the LORD. He said that Joshua was clothed in filthy garments, and Satan was standing at his right hand to resist him. The high priest in this scripture was the mediator,

How Did We Get Here From There and How Do We Get Back There From Here

and the representative of the people before God. According to verse 4, after the filthy garments were removed from Joshua, the LORD said that He caused Joshua's iniquity to pass from him. This scripture leads me to conclude that Joshua's filthy state and condition was prophetically, the collective, or corporate state and condition of the whole nation.

In verse 5, the LORD called for a new mitre to be put on Joshua's head, and then he was clothed with a change of garments. The LORD told him that if he would walk in His ways, and keep His charge, then he would judge the LORD's house. He told Joshua that He would give him places to walk among those that stood by. If I were to follow through with my previous conclusion, it would be consistent to say that the condition and state of the high priest, matched the state and condition of five of the churches in Revelation 2, which is prophetic of the Body of Christ in our times.

Our robe of righteousness, and our garment of praise was made filthy by the corruption of religion, and the spirit of worldliness. Our mitre/mind of Christ was polluted by the wisdom of the world, and the deceit of religion. God is going to raise up apostolic and prophetic voices by which He will give us a change of garments. The scripture says, that the House of God is built upon the apostles and prophets, with Jesus Christ Himself being the chief cornerstone. He will cause them to put a new or changed mitre/mind on our head, which speaks of the renewed mind of Christ. They will take off the old garment, which speaks of the filthy garments of religion and worldliness, and clothe us with new garments, which speaks of righteousness.

In 1 Corinthians 1:30-31, we are told that Christ is our sanctification and righteousness. In Romans 13:14, we are told to clothe ourselves with the LORD Jesus Christ (NIV). So if Christ is our righteousness, when we are clothed with Christ, or we put on Christ, we are being clothed with the garment of righteousness, which conveys a change of heart. This speaks of God's accepted repentance, because when we change our heart, and our mind, it causes us to turn, or walk in a new direction. This will cause the Body of Christ to regain our Christ centered identity, which will cause us to walk in God's ways, and keep His charge, based upon a renewed relationship.

Jesus Christ was the voice of God to those seven expressions of the Body of Christ. God is going to raise up in our times, voices who will cry out against the garments of religion and worldliness that His Body is clothed with. They will remove those clothing and replace them with the garments of intimacy, fellowship, and communion, otherwise known as the garment of relationship. He is going to raise up some

How Did We Get Here From There and How Do We Get Back There From Here

Elijah's, who will call for the repairing of the altar and a return to the LORD. He is going to raise up some Jeremiah's, who will root out, pull down, destroy, throw down, then build, and plant. He is going to raise up some Nehemiah's, who will be concerned about the House/Body of the LORD, because they will see with the eyes of God, and discern with His heart, the state and condition of His house, and its need of repair. He will also raise up some Daniel's, who will be able to understand the times and seasons. They will then begin to send up prayers, petitions, supplications, and intercession of confession and repentance, for the release of God's people from Babylonian captivity.

Although the name Gehazi meant valley of vision, he was blinded by his lust of carnality for silver, gold, and garments. When Elijah complained to God that all Israel had backslid, and were worshiping Baal, God informed him that He had a remnant who had not kissed the hand of Baal, or bowed to worship him. God is raising up voices to call for His remnant. He is raising up voices to call out for those who are on the LORD's side. The word *remnant* means a small piece or amount of something that is left from a larger original piece, or a small surviving group. He will call forth the remnant, and give them a new change of garment. He will wash them and anoint their eyes.

Prophetic Release

I heard the Lord saying that they shall be like chaste virgins again unto me, for I will forgive their iniquities. For the iniquity of my people am I grieved, but in their healing shall I rejoice. I shall rebuild what has been torn down, and strengthen what has been shaken. I shall raise up my repairers of the breach, and them who shall restore paths for my people to dwell in. The foundation shall be sure once again, for I the LORD, am its builder. The latter days of my house shall be greater than the former days of its beginning. No more shall the old men cry and the young men rejoice, but in my Glory they shall rejoice together. No more shall my people keep quiet, or hold their peace because of the iniquity of their unrighteousness. No more shall silence fill my house, for my glory shall be the voice of my people. Restoring I shall restore, for their righteousness shall be of me. Voices that have never been heard before in the earth, shall now be heard, for the remnant of my people shall go forth as a man of war, and as a lion to the prey. I shall lift the weight of ungodliness from off the shoulder of my people, and I shall rest the weight of my glory upon them. The fire of the LORD shall go before them, to consume their opposition and to destroy their fear. No more shall my people be asked "where is their God?" In my glory I shall answer for you, and in my might I shall silence them. If

How Did We Get Here From There and How Do We Get Back There From Here

the remnant of my people will allow me to stand up in their midst, then shall I be able to stand up for them. A remnant shall return and serve me before my return. I call to you my people, to be a part of my remnant, for they have I chosen to enter in with me. My name shall be called The LORD of the Remnant. The remnant of my people shall be likened to a new generation unto me. In my glory shall I visit them, in like manner as I visited Elizabeth and Mary.

The Intimacy, Purpose and Power of Prayer

Chapter 19

How the Deception was Carried Out

Everything that is written in this book concerning the power and gifting of the early Community of New Covenant Believers, is a powerful and dynamic testimony and tangible evidence of what our heavenly Father is able to do through His redeemed, yielded, faithful and surrendered vessels. I stated earlier that worldliness and religion was responsible for their demise. In wrapping up this book, I want to go into some detail as to how the enemy was able to accomplish his agenda through those two avenues. The principle is this. If you do not know where you lost it, you will not know where to find it. If you do not know how it was done, then you will not know how to undo it. If you do not know how you got lost, then you will not know how to retrace your steps in finding your way back.

Natural Babylon carried away God's people into Babylonian captivity. Spiritual Babylon has done the very same thing to the Body of Christ (spiritual Israel of God). Natural Babylon stole the gifts and treasures from the temple or House of God. We see this in 2 Chronicles 36:18 where it states *"And all the vessels of the house of God, great and small, and the treasures of the house of the LORD, and the treasures of the king, and of his princes; all these he brought to Babylon."* Spiritual Babylon has done the exact same thing. For example, in Ephesians 4:11, it states that when Jesus ascended, He gave gifts to His House/Temple/Body. He gave some apostles, some prophets, some evangelists, some pastors and teachers.

In 2 Corinthians 4:7, we are told that Christ has put heavenly his treasure in earthen vessels. The spirit of Babylon have committed virtual theft of these gifts by diluting their effectiveness. In stealing these gifts, they were downgraded in functionality from being actively demonstrated, to being a mere shadow of themselves. The ones who possessed these gifts went from being active participators, to side line spectators. These gifts are recognized and accepted today, but to a very limited degree. They do not operate to the same extent or degree that God intended. There is no demonstration of the power of these gifts at the level that was evident in the life of the early Community of New Covenant Believers.

In 1 Kings 14:25-27, we are told that after Shishak, of Egypt, raided the Temple of Solomon, and carried off all the gold and treasures, Rehoboam then replaced the gold shields with brass ones. Gold has a much higher melting point than brass (engineersedge.com). This means that it can endure more heat before changing from solid to liquid. In Ephesians 6:16, Paul speaks about the shield of faith that is used to quench the fiery dart of the wicked. Much like the gold shields that were replaced by brass shields in Solomon's temple, the pure solid gold shield of faith, has the capacity to withstand the intense heat of doubt and skepticism, than brass faith. Brass has a similar look to gold, but a smaller capacity to withstand the same amount of heat. Upon close examination, and trial by fire, this brass shield of faith, when targeted by the fiery darts of the wicked, will fail. That is why our faith is operating on a lesser level, because the faith that allows us to operate in miracles, signs, and wonders, was taken. What has been put in its place is intellectual brass faith.

In Romans 8:18, Paul tells us that there is a glory in us to be revealed. The only problem is that it first has to return, before it can be revealed. Gold in scripture speaks of glory. The gifts that are currently in the Body of Christ, in our times, is operating at brass level, which is a third rate level. The order of superiority of these metals is gold, silver, and brass. God intended for these gifts to operate on the glory level.

It was natural Judah that was taken into captivity, and it was to spiritual Babylon that spiritual Judah was taken. In 1 Peter 2:9, it states that we are to show forth the praises of Him who have called us out of darkness in to His marvelous light. Judah means praise. The Body of Christ is spiritual Judah, because we are the praise of God. When spiritual Judah was taken away by spiritual Babylon, they were replaced by counterfeits appearing as the real thing.

The Intimacy, Purpose and Power of Prayer

When Nebuchadnezzar of Babylon took away Judah, he replaced them in the land with other peoples, who then passed themselves off as Jews, and descendants of Abraham, Isaac, and Jacob. This is where the story, or narrative of the Samaritans originated. That is why Jesus said to the church in Revelation 3:9, that there are those who call themselves Jews, but are found to be liars. He said that there are those who call themselves Jews, but are of the synagogue of Satan. The spirits of Jezebel, Balaam, and the Nicolaitans are all Babylonian spirits. Together, they have triumphed over, and stolen from God's house. In John 10:10, Jesus said that the devil comes only to steal, kill and destroy.

The Nicolaitans conquered and subdued the people. They robbed God's people of their priesthood. This action created the division of clergy and laity in the Body of Christ. The people of God could no longer exercise their Christ given rights to go boldly to the Throne of Grace. Instead of going before Him as His priest, they were forced to go through a man-made system. Babylon stole the spirit of the Bereans from the Body of Christ. In Acts 17:11, we are told that the Bereans received the word with all readiness of mind, and searched the scriptures daily, to ascertain whether those things that the Apostles were preaching, were true. They had an investigative mind and were in search of truth. They examined the scriptures for themselves. They did not leave it up to others, not even the Apostles. The "liturgy" or teaching, eventually came to be done in Latin, so the people had to depend on the priest to read the word and interpret it for them. They kept the people ignorant and illiterate, so they would have no other choice but to depend on them. In other words, spiritual Babylon dummied down God's people.

The spirit of Jezebel was a lying, stealing, murderous and deceitful spirit. We read the narrative in 1 Kings 21, how Ahab the king of Israel wanted the vineyard of Naboth, because it was supposedly next to his palace. Naboth refused to sell it to him, so he got quite depressed. When his wife found out that it was because Naboth refused to sell him his vineyard, she conspired against Naboth by having people bear false witness against him, that he had blasphemed God and the king. She instructed them, to whom the letter was sent, to take Naboth out and stone him that he may die. They followed the instructions of Jezebel, and Naboth was murdered.

The spirit of Baalam was a covetous and undermining spirit. He instructed Balak the king of Moab how to undermine the people of God, so as to get them to sin against God, and ensure certain judgment, in order to gain money. Babylon stole the compassion and passion of the cross from the heart of God's people and extinguished their fire. They made a religion out of the cross, and took the fulfillment of a powerful event and made it a powerless event, and a mere narrative within an historical context. By doing this, they robbed the cross of its level of power and impact that Jesus' sacrifice deposited in, and empowered the cross with. These three Babylonian spirits subverted the early Community of New Covenant Believers. The word subvert means *"to overturn or overthrow from the foundation; ruin; to pervert or corrupt by an undermining of morals, allegiance, or faith."* That is why Jesus was so fierce and adamant in His letters to the seven churches.

Although a remnant did escape out of Babylon during the age of the reformation, they brought with them some habits and practices of Babylon. For example the people of God in our times do not spend time searching out, examining, or investigating the word of God for themselves. They depend on the preacher, pastor, or teacher to explain what the word of God is saying, or what it means. Worship was seen as a Sunday religious experience, and not an everyday way of life unto God. As a result, Sunday became the god that is worshipped instead of one of the days in which God is worshipped. The Body of Christ is not doing the work of the ministry through the operation of the Body gifts. That has been abandoned and set as the responsibility of the head gifts. As a result, men are being idolized and esteemed beyond measure, while the rest of the Body looks on. This will not be for long, because when the remnant shall return from Babylon, God shall restore the gifts, the vessels, the treasure, the gold and the silver, that were taken from out of His House/Temple/Body. He will call his house back to order, and His body back into alignment, that it may function and operate according to His original intent and design. As He has done it for natural Judah, in Ezra 1:7, so shall He likewise do it for spiritual Judah. He will *"return, and will build again the tabernacle of David, which is fallen down; and I will build again the ruins thereof, and I will set it up.*" (Acts 15:16). Therefore, "*Those the LORD has rescued will return. They will enter Zion with singing; everlasting joy will crown their heads. Gladness and joy will overtake them, and sorrow and sighing will flee away*" (Isaiah 51:11, NIV).

"*He that goeth forth and weepeth, bearing precious seed, shall doubtless come again with rejoicing, bringing his sheaves with him*" (Psalm 126:6).

The Intimacy, Purpose and Power of Prayer

My Story

I maintain a relationship, fellowship and communion based life of prayer not because my religion, denomination or church told me that I have to. Neither do I pray out of a legalistic or ritualistic obligation. I do so because my Heavenly Father shared with me directly, why it is important for me to have such a lifestyle.

In the early years of my walk with the LORD, I spent my time doing a lot of things. Praying was, by far, not one of them. I went to bed one night and had this horrible dream. I dreamt that I was standing outside of my church, and a large, grotesque, scary, beastly looking creature appeared before me. It had the form and features of a man. It kinda growled at me, while showing its beast-like fangs. As it began to move towards me, I began to rebuke it in Jesus name. It did not stop. All it did was laugh at me, and kept advancing toward me. I jumped out of my sleep before I could know what would happen next. I perceived that my Heavenly Father was showing me that because the kingdom of darkness knew that I had no real relationship with him, the devil knew that I had no power or authority, and was not afraid of me. He did not take me serious.

After that experience, I thrusted myself into building up, and sustaining a serious lifestyle of praying and fasting. One year later, almost to the date, I had the same dream again. That same grotesque creature began to move toward me again. This time, as I rebuked it in Jesus name, it stopped suddenly in its tracks, turned around and began to walk away from me. As it walked away, it kept looking back at me with such evil and hatred in its eyes. It was as if it wanted to turn back and literally tear me to shreds.

As I maintained that lifestyle of fellowship with my Heavenly Father, I began to grow spiritually. I knew that my spirit was growing, because I could literally feel as if my spirit was expanding, stretching, and being enlarged on the inside of my body. A few years later, I dreamt that I was being chased by two vicious demon-like dogs. As I ran, they began to chase me. This continued for a while. The next thing I knew, even though my feet were still in the running motion on the ground, I began to lift off the ground, and was now running in the air. As I looked down, I realized that I had been lifted way up above those demonic creatures. All that they could do at that point was to stop chasing me, and just kept barking. This experience again was another way that God was showing me how much I was growing.

My Story

The key to having a lifestyle of prayer, is not to only have a desire to pray, but it is to have a desire and longing for the Father, and an appetite, and hunger for the Kingdom of God, and His righteousness. Once we crave for God in that way, He will fill us with a passion and an insatiable appetite that will cause us to be in the pursuit, and courtship of His presence. I remembered how for a season, while growing up in God, I would lock myself in church and cry out in prayer all night for the Kingdom of God. I would leave my wife and children on Fridays at 11:00 pm and pray all night until 6 am. Then I would return on Saturday at 11:00 pm and pray all night until 6 a.m. Sunday morning. I would leave and go home to get ready for service, then return before anyone else, to open up the church, and to clean up outside of the building. This I did for many years, which was unknown to my pastor or members of the congregation. I did not bring a blanket, pillow or snacks. I was not trying to comfort or pamper the flesh, or to feed it. I went there to seek God, and that was what I spent my time doing. I paced back and forth, while praying all night. As a result of my hunger and thirst for God, I would embark upon seasons of fasting and prayer. Sometimes I would fast three days, and other times I would fast seven days. One year I went on twenty one days of fasting and prayer. I was working in a factory at the time, and I did not take a day off during those twenty one days. There were other times, however, where I did take vacation time off just so I could seek God in fasting and prayer. I was so serious about seeking God that I would mark the days that I was going to fast on a calendar.

The Intimacy, Purpose and Power of Prayer

I did this so that when the time was close for me to fast, I would begin to prepare my heart, mind and body. When I had to plan to do other things, I would plan around my fasting times. That meant that my fasting took precedence. I would fast when I knew that my favorite television show was going to be airing for the last time for the season, or when it was returning for its season premier. It was my way of disciplining my flesh and denying it of its cravings. My passion or heart for fasting and prayer did not come from a bible verse or sermon. It came directly from my Heavenly Father.

One day, I was on three days of fasting and prayer while at work. At the time, I worked as a book binder at a printing and publishing company. As I raised myself up, from bending down, to place a box of books onto a plastic pallet, I saw a vision that was cast on the wall before me. It seemed as if it was there for five minutes and five seconds simultaneously. I saw in the vision, a man dressed in a black suit, and a white shirt. He had a large stomach. He was lying flat on his back with both of his hands pressed up against his side, while looking up into the ceiling. All around him was dark, but there was what seemed like a stage light above him, shining directly down on him. He showed no sign of life or consciousness. I wondered to myself, while asking the LORD at the same time, "What does this vision mean?" He said to me plainly, "That is what happens to the flesh when you fast." He continued to say that "when a person dies, their spirit is released from the body, and when we fast, it slays our flesh, which causes our spirit to rise in the realms of God."

He then asked me this question. "Why when those men work on the train tracks they are not electrocuted?" He said it is because they are wearing protective gear, which does not conduct energy and as a result the current is not able to get through to or penetrate their bodies. He said that in like manner, our flesh, which is our protective gear, covers our spirit and does not allow the power of His presence to get through to our spirit. So when we fast, we are removing the blockage or hindrance that keeps us from reaching the Father, and Him from reaching us.

I want to take a moment to make something emphatically clear. It does not matter what God shows you, tells you where He wants to take you, or what He wants to do in your life. You will never get there on your own or by yourself. God will connect you to the right people, or surround you with the right relationships that you will need, to help you get to your place of destiny. It is in that place, where He has commanded your blessing, provision, anointing, purpose and assignment.

It did not matter the passion, hunger, zeal or desire that I had, or the vision or dreams that my Heavenly Father gave me. It was not "Just me and Jesus" on this path. God placed people in my life to challenge me, to press me, to stretch me, and to aim me. He put people in my life to help fan the flames. He connected me to people who would leave an indelible mark and a lasting impression upon the canvas of my heart. These were people who made life impacting deposits and impartations within the repository of my spirit, and within the corridors of my mind.

I came to faith in Christ at the young age of about fifteen years old, by the witness of a sister in Christ who was a great woman of prayer, and a strong intercessor. I would attend prayer meetings at her home, with her children and a few other brethren. We had these meetings every Monday night at 7:30 pm. It was on one of these nights of prayer that God filled me with the baptism of the Holy Spirit. I continued to attend prayer at her home until I relocated from Canada to the United States. She deposited in me a passion for prayer and seeking God.

When I came to the United States, the LORD connected me with a lifelong friend and covenant brother. We grew up together from our teenage years in the same ministry and under the leadership of the same pastor. I watched him over the years, how he grew and matured in God. I watched how God began to raise him up, and use him mightily. I bore witness to his faithfulness, passion, heart and love for God. When I would go before the Father in my times of fellowship

My Story

and communion, I would tell him that I do not want my brother's gifting, ministry, or anointing. I would tell God, that I instead wanted to have the same heart, passion, love, faithfulness, commitment, and zeal for God like he had. He spoke timely wisdom and sound counsel into my spirit. It was not so much what he spoke to me from behind the pulpit that had the greatest impact on me. It was what he spoke to me through the example of his life. He directed me, equipped me, activated me, aimed me, and prepared me for my destiny and my God ordained assignment. The LORD raised up this my brother, to be my very respected and honorable spiritual father, and mentor, in the person of Bishop Roderick Roberts. I also pay great homage to my friend, the late Arlene Hope Roberts. I learned to pray and intercede for my three children, by listening to her pray and intercede for her three children. I also pay homage to my spiritual mother, Doreen Roberts. I honor her for the respect and honor that she has shown to our late mother, and the legacy that she left behind. I also pay her great homage for being to our spiritual father, who he needs her to be, so that he may be to the flock, who God has purposed him to be.

I would like to mention one other name in the person of Bishop Hugh Daniel Smith. He was a great help in my family and I finally relocating to Florida, even though we knew by the word of the LORD, that it was His will for us to move. The challenge and push that I needed to finally step out by faith and begin to embark, and act upon the will of the LORD, came from him. The impact that these individuals especially, and others, have had on my life, have helped to position and posture me, for the cause, for which I have been brought to the kingdom. It prepared me to answer the call of my destiny, which I received at about 15 years old.

Such impact and influence have brought me to a place in my walk and relationship with the LORD, where I am able to hear Him for myself, know what He has called me to do, know the mantle that He has placed upon my life, know the giftings that He has given me to carry out my assignment, and to know the place of my assignment. All of these individuals have contributed to the reason why I am writing this book. The moral of my story is this simple truth. It does not matter how great you may become, how much God may use you, or how far you may reach in God. Never forget those relationships that God used to help get you there. Paul said in 1 Corinthians 11:1, that we should be followers of him, even as also he is of Christ. The Contemporary English Version says you must follow my example, as I follow the example of Christ. Always look for people who you know love God, and have a heart for the things of God, who are examples that you can pattern your life after. They are people who you can follow as they follow Christ.

Why I Wrote This Book

I was never really interested in writing a book of any sort. I felt about writing a book the same way I felt about ministry. I was not interested in doing either of them. My mindset was that there were enough preachers in the Body of Christ. I was set on taking up another profession. Preaching was not something I wanted to do. As a result, I ran from it for about 18 or so years, until one day I was reading Act 9, where the LORD called Paul on the road of Damascus. Paul asked "who art thou LORD what will thou have me to do?" As soon as I got through reading this passage, the LORD stopped me dead in my tracts, and said, "See. I called Paul, and he asked me what I would have him to do. I am calling you, and you are resisting arrest." The LORD used the calling of Paul to convict me concerning my calling. I decided that I could no longer pretend, or act like I did not know that there was a calling on my life. As a result, I began to prepare myself, through the process of time, for ministry.

Over the course of time, I grew in wisdom, stature, and status in my walk with the LORD. I am currently writing this book from my place in ministry. I had been writing many manuscripts for years, but I really did not have book publishing on my mind. I received prophecies concerning writing, but I still was never sold on the idea. I did not have the desire, will, or motivation to write, like I stated earlier. My mindset was that there were enough writers and books out there. I did not want to write just to write. I did not want to write just to make money from the books. I did not want to write in order to attain some kind of status as an author. I did not want to write, because I was not convinced that I really had anything of value to say, that would justify people paying money for my book. There were certain individuals who kept encouraging me to write. I did keep writing, but I would also keep asking the LORD, what am I going to do with all these writing materials. The manuscripts that I wrote over the years, just languished on my ipad and laptop.

A covenant brother of mine, name Samuel Broomes was one of those individuals who kept encouraging me to write. I moved from NY to Florida, but more times than not, whenever we spoke on the phone, we never ended our conversation without him asking me how the writing was coming along, or if I had done any writing lately. It was his way of pushing me, and also holding me accountable. Afterward, I would get this rush of energy and desire to write, sometimes for weeks at a time. The other individual who also had a hand in me finally deciding to write, was Elder Rowley. Just before relocating from New York to Florida, one of the last things that he said to me was to make sure that you keep writing. He said that your provision and your blessing is in your hand.

Why I wrote this Book

The other person who had the greatest impact in me writing, is my competent, well capable, and equal counterpart, my help-meet, Paulette. She could always see greatness in me, even when I could not see it. She always believed in me, when I could not see what was in me to believe in. She would keep pushing me, by asking me when I was going to start writing again, or when I planned on finishing the first manuscript. I would keep giving her, what I now consider to be nothing but excuses. Six months after moving to Florida, as we sat home, we began to discuss the manuscripts that I was working on. She was really pressing the issue, to the point where I got respectfully annoyed. I wrote down the contact information for a publishing company that I saw advertising on the television. After writing down the number, I put the paper down with the intent to call, but never really gave it any priority. After she realized that I still had not called the number as yet, she pressed me until I did. After a period of a day or two, the LORD said to me, He allowed her to press me, and to light the fire under me, because I was comfortable in just writing the manuscripts. He said that even though I was writing, I still could not see having my books published. He said that he had to use her to move the blockage, and the limitations from off of my mind. He said, that as long as I had those limitations on my mind, he was unable to share with me why I had to write and publish my books. He said to me, that because other people wrote their books, I was able to read them, which helped me to get to where I am in my walk, and relationship with Him now. He went on to say, that this is why I have to write my books, so that others may read it, and get to the next level in their walk with Him. He said that this book is a manual to the next generation. It will raise up a David like generation unto Him. It will introduce His people into a new dimension of Him. It will bring about a revolution in their thinking. They will learn how to practice entering into His Presence. They will learn how to be culture carriers of His Presence. Because their hearts, minds, and spirits will be prepared to receive more, He will also be prepared to release more into them.

As a result of what the LORD spoke to me, I wrote this book from start to finish in about two months. So, I again want to truly thank everyone who pushed me and encouraged me to write. I would also like to thank those who made material contributions in my life, through their examples, their deposits, their lasting impressions, and the impact that they have made on my life. I hope to transfer some of the same into your life that you may also one day, be able to pass on the same effect into the lives of countless others.

Why I wrote this Book

What has been written in this book is by no means an exhaustive discussion about prayer. It was written from a personal and experiential point of view.

References

Augustyn, A. (2019). Potential energy. Retrieved from
    https://www.britannica.com/science/potential-energy

Augustyn, A. (2019). Kinetic energy. Retrieved from
    https://www.britannica.com/science/kinetic-energy

Clin Haematol. (1985). Blood volume changes in normal
    pregnancy, 14(3), pp.601-12. Retrieved from
    https://www.ncbi.nlm.nih.gov/pubmed/4075604

Conception: From Egg to Embryo. (2019). Retrieved from
    https://www.webmd.com/baby/ss/slideshow-conception

Conte, R. (2012). What do Pontifex and Pontifex Maximus
    mean?. Retrieved December 2018 from
    https://ronconte.com/2012/12/03/what-do-pontifex-and-
    pontifex-maximus-mean/

Gregersen, E. (2019). Energy. Retrieved from
    https://www.britannica.com/science/energy

Healthy Lifestyle. Pregnancy week by week. (Heart
    conditions and pregnancy: Know the risks). (2017).
    Rertieved from
    https://www.mayoclinic.org/healthy-lifestyle/pregnancy-
    week-by-week/in-depth/pregnancy/art-20045977

Hirschman, D. (2017). What Am I? Attitude Indicator. Keep
    The Blue Side Up. Retrieved from
    https://www.aopa.org/news-and-media/all-ne
    ws/2017/november/flight-training-magazine/what-am-i-

attitude-indicator

International travel and health. (n.d.). World Health
    Organization. Retrieved from
    https://www.who.int/ith/mode_of_travel/cab/en/

Metal Melting Temperatures. (2019). Retrieved from
    https://www.engineersedge.com/materials/metal_melting_t
    emperatures_13214.htm

Origin of the Pope. (n.d.). Retrieved January 2019 from
    http://www.biblestudy.org/basicart/origin-of-the-title-of-
    pope-as-head-of-catholic-church.html

Pope Seated On Satan's Throne. (n.d.). Hope of Israel
    Ministries. Retrieved from http://hope-of-
    israel.org/pope.htm

Pregnancy and Conception. (2018). Retrieved from
    https://www.webmd.com/baby/understanding-conception#1

Rogers, K. (2019). Thermal energy. Retrieved from
    https://www.britannica.com/science/thermal-energy

Reynolds, P. (n.d.). The Lumberjack Story. Retrieved from
    http://qatc.org/winter-2017-connection/the-lumberjack-
    story/

Sperm Physiology. (2019). Rertieved from
    https://www.britannica.com/science/sperm

Strong's Exhaustive Concordance Online:
    https://biblehub.com/strongs.htm
    https://www.biblestudytools.com/concordances/strongs
    -exhaustive-concordance/
    https://www.bibletools.org/

The Nicolaitans. (n.d.). Retrieved January 2019 from
    http://www.biblestudy.org/basicart/why-does-god-hate-
    practices-of-the-nicolaitans.html

The Olympic Flame. (2016). Retrieved from
    https://www.olympic.org/news/the-amazing-story-of-the-
    olympic-flame

The Olympic Torch Relay. (n.d.). Retrieved February 2019
    from https://www.olympic.org/olympic-torch-relay

Walvoord, J.F. (2008). The Letters To Ephesus, Smyrna,
    Pergamos, And Thyatira. Bible.org. Retrieved from
    https://bible.org/seriespage/2-letters-ephesus-smyrna-
    pergamos-and-thyatira

What Is Energy? Explained. (2018). Retrieved from
    https://www.eia.gov/energyexplained/index.php?page=abou
    t_home

What is the concept of the vicarious atonement? (n.d.). *Got
    Questions*. Retrieved from
    https://www.gotquestions.org/vicarious-atonement.html

What is the umbilical cord? (2018). *NHS*. Retrieved
    February 2019 from https://www.nhs.uk/common-health-
    questions/pregnancy/what-is-the-umbilical-cord/

Who Were the Nicolaitans, And What Was Their Doctrine
    and Deeds? (2016). Retrieved March 2019 from
    https://renner.org/who-were-nicolaitans-what-was-
    doctrine-deeds/

Study Notes

Published by

Divine { } Word
Impact

gcrumbie@divinewordimpact.org

"*Thy word is a lamp unto my feet, and a light unto my path.*"

Made in the USA
Columbia, SC
07 June 2021

39369565R00111